Principles of Big Data

Principles of Big Data

Alvin Albuero De Luna

ARCLER
PRESS

www.arclerpress.com

Principles of Big Data

Alvin Albuero De Luna

Arcler Press
224 Shoreacres Road
Burlington, ON L7L 2H2
Canada
www.arclerpress.com
Email: orders@arclereducation.com

ISBN: 978-1-77407-622-4 (Hardcover)

ABOUT THE AUTHOR

Alvin Albuero De Luna is an instructor at a Premier University in the Province of Laguna, Philippines - the Laguna State Polytechnic University (LSPU). He finished his Bachelor's degree in Information Technology at STI College and took his Master of Science in Information Technology at LSPU. He isnhandling Programming Languages, Cyber Security, Discrete Mathematics, CAD, and other Computer related courses under the College of Computer Studies

TABLE OF CONTENTS

LIST OF ABBREVIATIONS

ABAP	Advanced Business Application Programming
AHC	agglomerative hierarchical clustering
ARL	association rule learning
BI	business intelligence
CAGR	compound annual growth rate
CCE	Coca-Cola Enterprises
CRM	customer relationship management
DAML	DARPA agent markup language
DARPA	defense advanced research projects agency
DSS	decision support systems
EAI	enterprise application integration
EDR	enterprise data replication
EII	enterprise information integration
ETL	extract, transform, and load
GMMs	Gaussian mixture models
HDD	hard disk drives
IoT	internet of things
iPaaS	integration platform as a service
MDM	master data management
NLP	natural language processing
NOAA	National Oceanic and Atmospheric Administration
OTP	on time performance
PCA	principal component analysis
RDF	resource description framework
SMO	strategic marketing organization

SSD	solid state drives
STAN	structural analysis
SVM	support vector machine

PREFACE

'Principles of Big Data' has been created and written to make the readers aware about the various aspects related to Big Data, which may be used by the users to help them with analysis of the various situations and processes, so that they can deduce a logical conclusion from that data or information. The field of data is increasing and advancing at a very rapid pace and is growing in an exponential way to accommodate more and more data and information in it.

This developing field has a lot to offer for the users to provide them with insights on the market trends, consumer behavior, manufacturing processes, occurrence of errors and situations and various other fields. Big Data helps to handle the enormous amounts of data and information and makes it possible for the analysts to get some conclusive insights on the subject they may be analyzing.

To get a good understanding of Big Data, it may be a good idea to first understand the principles that Big Data is based on and its meaning. The manual defines Big Data for the readers and explains the various characteristics of Big Data. It makes them aware of the different kinds of analytics and their usage across various verticals.

The manual explains the readers the process of structuring the unstructured data and explains to them the concept of de-identification and the various techniques used in it. They are also informed about data scrubbing and further told the meaning of bad data. There are some approaches that can help improve the quality of data, which are mentioned in the manual. The manual also throws light on the ontologies and the advantages and disadvantages related to them. The manual also explains the process of data integration, discussing the various areas of data integration, its types, the challenges that lie in the integration process.

Further, the manual explains the process of regression and the various aspects related to the predictive learning model. It informs the readers about the different kinds of algorithms. The manual covers the various strategies that may be employed in the reduction of data and the methods involved in the process. It also explains the process of data visualization and the major considerations that may be taken for Big Data Analytics. The manual enlists various steps that are involved in the approach to analyze Big Data.

There is also a mention of the various legal issues related to the Big Data and also the societal ones. There is a focus on the various social issues that Big Data may help in addressing and a discussion about the future of Big Data and the trends that may be seen in the coming times.

This manual tries to give a complete insight into the principles and concepts of Big Data so that the professionals and the subject enthusiasts find it easy to understand the topic. The areas of topics mentioned above form a very short description of the kind of knowledge that is provided in the manual. I hope that the readers can achieve some good value with the information that has been provided in the manual. Any constructive criticism and feedback, is most welcome.

CHAPTER 1

Introduction to Big Data

LEARNING OBJECTIVE

In this chapter, you will learn about:

- The meaning of data and Big Data;
- The characteristics of Big Data;
- The actual description of Big Data Analytics;
- Different kinds of analytics in Big Data;
- The meaning of structured data;
- The meaning of unstructured data; and
- The process of structuring the unstructured data.

Keywords
Big data, Analytics, Velocity, Volume, Variety, Veracity, Variability, Value, Structured Data, Unstructured data, SQL

1.1. INTRODUCTION

Big Data is an evolving field and takes into account huge sets of data and information to be processed to provide insights on certain subject matters. The analysis done using Big Data acts as a great source from which business as well as informational insights can be taken. It can provide the companies with new opportunities to provide revenue to the extent which has not even been imagined, across various sectors and industries.

Big Data can be used to personalize the customer experience, mitigate the risks in a process, detect fraudulent situations, conduct internal operation analysis and various other valuable aspects, as the companies compete among themselves to have the best analytical operations in the modern world.

There are a lot of concepts in the field of Big Data. This manual aims to lay down the principles of Big Data and inform about the relevance of Big Data and its application in analysing various situations and events, to reach a comprehensive solution.

The main purpose of synthesizing data and processing it in the field of Big Data is basically to have a conclusive insight on a certain subject and, if possible, find some appropriate ways to either deal with the situation of getting an advantage from it.

Big data is a huge field and involves big datasets and operations that are employed in handling the data. The various kinds of analyses help the users to derive a conclusion or result from the data and also helps in building strategies, thus, providing the desired profits to them. Big data can help in improving customer service for a business, making the operations in business more efficient, helps the management to make better and informed decisions and suggest a line of action to the users.

For a better understanding of the Big Data, one must have a basic understanding of the following:

- Concept of Big Data;
- Structuring of the Unstructured Data;
- The Identifier System;
- Data Integration in Big Data;
- Interfaces to Big Data Resources;
- Big Data Techniques;
- Approaches to Big Data Analysis;
- The Legal Obligations in Big Data; and
- The Societal Issues in Big Data.

1.2. CONCEPT OF BIG DATA

Big Data is a term that is used for the various modern strategies and technologies which may be employed to collect data, organize it and process it to provide specific insights and conclusions from the datasets of huge sizes.

However, it is not a recently developed problem that the operations on data go beyond the capacity of a computer to compute or store. Additionally, the scale at which the data computing is being done, the value it generates and its capacity to be accepted universally, has gone up sharply in the last few years.

1.3. WHAT IS DATA?

Data may be defined as the various quantities, symbols or characters that are focused on, by the computer to perform the operations and that may be transmitted by the computing systems in the form of electrical signals and stored on various devices that may be mechanical, optical or magnetic in nature.

1.4. WHAT IS BIG DATA?

Big Data may be considered as data itself, although in an extremely enlarged way. The term Big Data may be used to denote a large pool of data, which tends to grow with time in an exponential manner.

This may imply that Big Data is found on such a large scale and with so many complexities, that it becomes next to impossible to compute this data or store it using the conventional tools of data management.

1.5. THE BIG DATA SYSTEMS ARE DIFFERENT

The fundamentals that are involved with the computation and storage of Big Data are the same as that involved with the operation of data sets of any size. The difference arises when factors such as the speed of processing the data and its ingestion, the enormity of the scale and the various characteristics that pertain to data at every stage of the process, come into play and pose some significant challenges at the time of finding the solutions.

The main aim of the systems pertaining to big data is to be able to provide insights and conclusions from the huge volumes of the data, which may be existing in mixed ways, as it would not be possible employing the traditional methods of data handling.

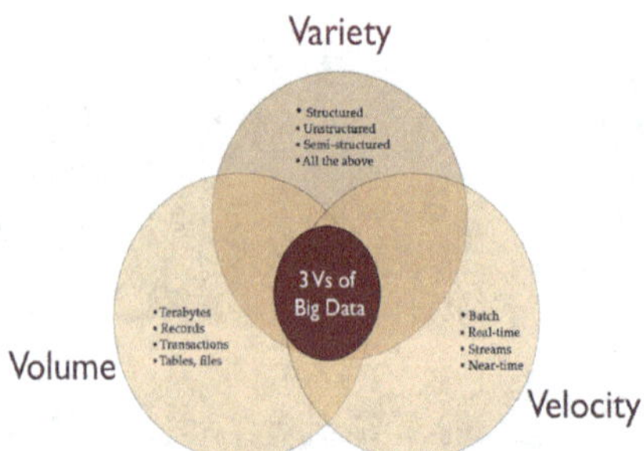

The first time, various characteristics of Big Data were presented was in 2001, when Gartner came up with 'the three Vs of Big Data' to describe it, differentiating it from the other forms of processing of data. These Vs are given as:

1.5.1. Volume

The Big Data systems may be defined by the scale of the information and data operated, itself.

The datasets pertaining to Big Data can have much greater scales as compared to the datasets that have been there traditionally. This requires an increased amount of effort and thinking at every step of the life cycle involving the processing and storage of data.

Generally, the requirements of the work to be done are found to be quite more than what a single computer can do. This gives rise to the challenge posed in the allocation, collection, and the coordination of resources, to be performed on a group of computers. Here, the various algorithms and the process of cluster management, which aims at breaking down the data and tasks into smaller fragments, assumes increased importance.

1.5.2. Velocity

The speed at which the data travels through the system, is another characteristic that makes Big Data different from the other kind of data systems. The data may be coming into the whole system through various sources. This data is generally required to be processed in a constrained amount of time for the purpose of getting insights and develop a certain perspective or conclusion about the system.

This kind of demand for the processing of data, has tempted the data scientists and professionals to change over to a real-time streaming system from that of a batch oriented one.

The addition of data has been a constant activity and simultaneously it is being processed, managed, and analysed so that the movement of new information keeps going on and the insights on the subject can be made available at the earliest, so that the relevance of the information is not lost with time.

The operations on these kinds of data require robust systems to be employed, that come with components that are available in good quality and quantity to deal with the failures that may come up along the data pipeline.

1.5.3. Variety

The problems arising in the Big Data are generally unique in nature as there is quite a large variety in both: the sources that are being processed and the quality related to them. The data, that is to be worked upon, can be taken up from the internal systems such as the application and server logs, external APIs, the feeds on social media and from various other providers such as the physical device sensors.

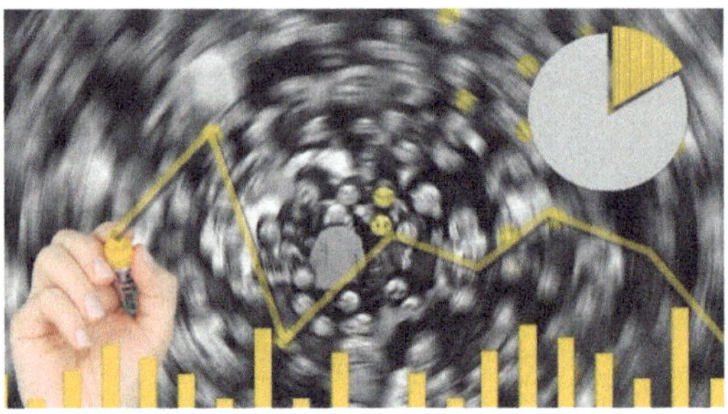

The data handling in Big Data aims to use and process the data that has some relevance and significance, and this does not depend on the origin of the data or information.

This is done by combining all that information to be grouped into a single system.

There can be quite a lot of significant variations in the formats and the types of media, which can be a characteristic of the Big Data systems.

In addition to the different kinds of text files and structured logs, the rich media are also dealt with, such as, the various images, video files and audio recordings.

The traditional data systems required the data that was entering the system pipeline to be in a properly labeled, organized, and formatted structure. On the other hand, the Big Data systems tend to inhibit the data in close appearance to its raw form and store it in a similar manner. In addition to this, the Big Data systems aim to reflect the changes and the transformations in the memory when the data is being processed.

1.5.4. The Other Characteristics of Big Data Systems

In addition to the three Vs, several people and various institutions have proposed that more Vs must be added to the characteristics of Big Data. However, these Vs pertain more to the challenges of big data than to its qualities.

These Vs may be given as:

- Veracity: There are some challenges that may arise in the evaluation of the quality of the data, which may come up due to the variety of sources and the various complexities in the processing. This in turn can degrade the quality of the final analysis of the data.
- Variability: There may be resulting variations in the quality due to the variation in data. There may be some additional resources required so that the data in lower quality may be identified, processed or filtered, for the purpose of being used in an appropriate manner.
- Value: Big Data eventually is required to deliver some value to the user. There are some instances in which the various systems and processes that are there in the system, are complicated in such a way that making use of the data to extract the actual value, can turn out to be quite difficult.

Learning Activity
Characteristics of Big Data
Find two cases that in your opinion, can differentiate between the importance of Big Data from that of normal in terms of volume and velocity, in the field of cloud storage.

1.6. BIG DATA ANALYTICS

The data stored in the system cannot generate value for the businesses and this holds true for all kinds of databases and technologies. However, the stored data, once synthesized properly, can be analysed to generate a good amount of value for the business. There is a wide range of technologies, approaches, and products that are exclusively related to big data like in-database analytics, in-memory analytics, and appliances.

Example of Big Data Analytics
The University of Alabama has more than 38,000 students and an ocean of data. In the past when there were no real solutions to analyze that much of data, some of them seem eduseless. Now, administrators are able to use analytics and data visualizations for this data to draw out patterns of students revolutionizing the university's operations, recruitment, and retention efforts.

1.6.1. The Meaning of Analytics

The analytics may be understood in a better way by knowing more about its origin. The first systems to help in the process of decision making were Decision Support Systems (DSS). After this, various decision support applications involving online analytical processing, executive information systems, and dashboards and scorecards came up to be used.

After all this, in the 1990s, an analyst at Gartner, Howard Dresner, made the term business intelligence (BI), popular among the professionals. BI is mainly defined as a broad category involving technologies, applications, and processes that have the purpose of collecting, storing, processing, and analyzing the data and information available to support the business professionals in making better decisions.

Thus, it is widely believed that analytics evolved primarily from BI. Analytics, can hence, be considered as an umbrella term, that involves all the data analysis applications.

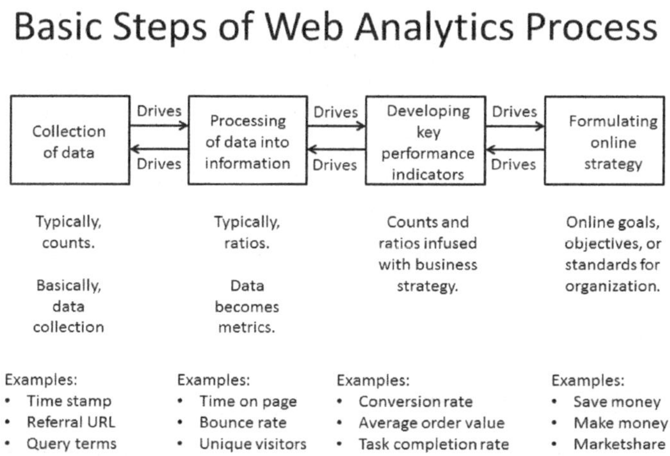

It can also be viewed as something that "gets data out" in the field of BI. Further, it is sometimes viewed as the use of "rocket science" algorithms, for the purpose of analyzing data.

Descriptive Analytics	The descriptive analytics which may involve reporting/OLAP, data visualizations, dashboards, and scorecards, have constituted the traditional BI applications for quite some time. The descriptive analytics inform the users about the things that have taken place in the past

Predictive Analysis	Another way to analyse is by finding the outcomes from predictive analysis, which may involve forecasts of future sales, on dashboards or scorecards. The methods pertaining to predictive analysis and the algorithms related to it like regression analysis, neural networks, and machine learning, have been there for quite some time now. There is a new kind of predictive analysis known as the Golden Path Analysis that aims to analyse the huge amounts of data pertaining to the behaviour of the customers. Using predictive analysis, a company can predict the behaviour of the customers, and can try and influence the behaviour, by using some kind of technique, such as introducing an offer on a product range.
Prescriptive Analysis	The third kind of analysis is that of the prescriptive analysis, which aims to inform the users about the things that are suggested to be done, like in the GPS system of a car. The prescriptive analysis can help find some optimal solutions for the allocation of the resources that are not enough in numbers.

1.6.2. Different Kinds of Data: Structured and Unstructured

1. What Is Structured Data?

The structured data is generally considered as quantitative data. This is such kind of data with which people are used to work with. Consider a data that actually fits precisely within the fixed fields as well as columns in relational databases and spreadsheets. Certain examples of the structured data consist of names, addresses, dates, stock information, credit card numbers, geolocation, and many more.

Structured data is very much organized and simply understood by the machine language. Those who are working within relational databases can input, then search and then manipulate the structured data rapidly. This is the most striking feature of the structured data.

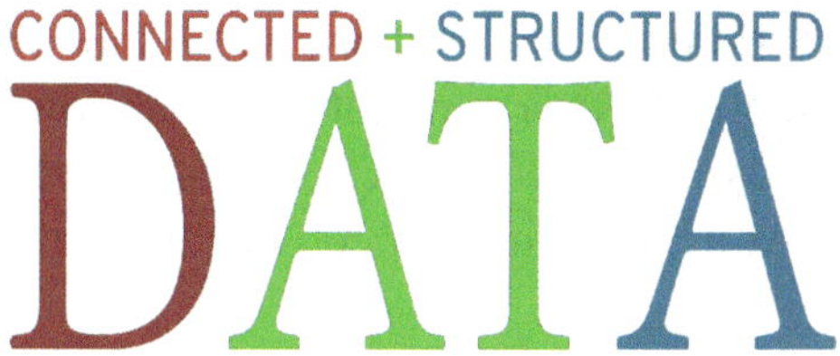

The programming language which is generally used for the management of structured data is known as structured query language (also called SQL). This language was basically developed by IBM during the early phase of 1970. SQL is mainly used for handling relationships in the databases.

Structured data often resides in relational databases (RDBMS). Fields store length-delineated data, ZIP codes, phone numbers, Social Security numbers, etc. Even the text strings of variable length such as names are also available in the records, making it a simple matter to search.

Data can be human generated or machine generated as long as the data is produced within an RDBMS structure. This kind of format is highly searchable with human generated queries as well as through algorithms using distinct data as well as field names, such as numeric or alphabetical, date or currency.

Common relational database applications with the structured data consist of airline reservation systems, sales transactions, inventory control, and ATM activity. SQL enables the queries on this kind of structured data within relational databases.

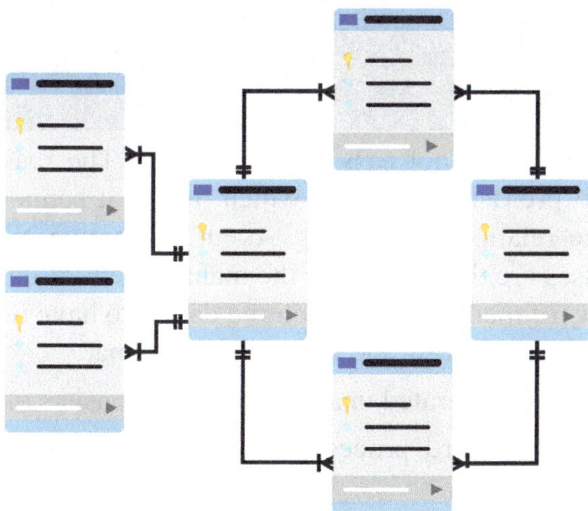

Some of the relational databases store unstructured data like customer relationship management (CRM) applications. The integration can be quite difficult as memo fields do not loan themselves to the queries related to a traditional database. At present, it has been observed that most of the CRM data is structured.

2. *What Is Unstructured Data?*

Unstructured data is completely different from structured data. Unstructured data has internal structure but it is not structured through pre-defined schema or data models. It can be textual or non-textual and humans or machine-generated. It can also be stored in a non-relational database such as No SQL.

Unstructured data is usually considered as qualitative data and it cannot be further processed and analyzed by using conventional tools as well as methods. Certain examples of unstructured data comprise audio, video, text, mobile activity, social media activity, surveillance imagery, satellite imagery and many more.

Examples of Unstructured Data in Real Life

Using deep learning, a system can be trained to recognize images and sounds. The systems learn from labeled examples in order to accurately classify new images or sounds. For instance, a computer can be trained to identify certain sounds that indicate that a motor is failing. This kind of application is being used in automobiles and aviation. Such technology is also being employed to classify business photos for online autosales or for identifying the products. A photo of an object to be sold in an online auction can be automatically labeled, for example. Image recognition is being put to work in medicine to classify mammograms as potentially cancer outstanding economics to understand disease markers.

Unstructured data is not easy to deconstruct. The reason behind this is that it has no pre-defined model, which means it cannot be effectively organized in the relational databases. As an alternative, non-relational or No SQL databases are the best fit for the management of unstructured data. Another key way of managing unstructured data is to have it flow into a data lake, letting it to be in its raw and unstructured format.

A typical human-generated unstructured data consists of:

- Text files: Word processing, presentations, spreadsheets, logs, email;

- Email: Email comprises some internal structure and the credit goes to its metadata. At times, it is referred to as semi-structured. Although, its message field is quite unstructured and the tools of traditional analytics cannot analyse it;
- Social Media: Data from Twitter, Facebook, LinkedIn;
- Website: Instagram, YouTube, photo sharing sites;
- Mobile data: Text messages and locations;
- Communications: Chat, phone recordings, IM, collaboration software;
- Media: MP3, audio, and video files, digital photos; and
- Business applications: MS Office documents and productivity applications.

A typical machine-generated unstructured data consists of:

- Satellite imagery: Weather data, military movements, land forms;
- Scientific data: Oil and gas exploration, seismic imagery, space exploration, atmospheric data;
- Digital surveillance: Surveillance photos and video; and
- Sensor data: Weather, traffic, oceanographic sensors.

Several enterprises would already comprise production-level Big Data as well as Internet of Things (IoT) infrastructure in place, if it were up to the executives of the enterprises today. It is unfortunate that it's not that simple. It turns out that the major hurdle that blocks the digital transformation is the method of managing the unstructured data that such fast-moving applications are likely to generate.

The issues and challenges involved in managing the unstructured data are known to the enterprises. However, to date the process of finding and analysing the amount of information hidden in chat rooms, emails, and various other forms of communication has been very clumsy to make it a critical consideration. If none of the individuals can access the data, then it signifies neither an advantage nor a disadvantage to anyone.

Although, this scenario is constantly changing, mainly because IoT as well as advanced analytics need this knowledge to be placed to better use. As some of the modern advances in the unstructured data management demonstrate, this is not just a matter of storage, but it is a matter of deep-dive data analysis as well as conditioning.

As per Gartner, object storage and the distributed file systems are at the frontline of the efforts so as to bring the structure to unstructured data. Start-ups as well as the established vendors are looking forward to the secret sauce that allows the scalable storage clustered file systems along with the object storage systems in order to meet the scalability and cost of the developing workloads.

Learning Activity
Unstructured Data
Find some instances, in which a company had to deal with unstructured data and the results it had, after it had been used. Also go through the various platforms on which structuring of data is carried out.

Distributed systems usually provide easy and fast access to the data for multiple hosts at the same time. On the other hand, the object storage provides the Restful APIs that have cloud solutions such as AWS and Open Stack. These solutions together can provide the enterprise with a cheap and economical way to make a proper infrastructure so as to take on heavy data loads.

Capturing and then storing data is one thing, but turning the stored data into a useful and effective resource is another. This process becomes more difficult once people enter the dynamic and rapidly moving world of the IoT. Therefore, various organizations are now turning to smart productivity assistants (Steve Olenski, Forbes Contributor).

With tools such as Work Chat and Slack, the collaborations are becoming easier. Knowledge workers require an effective way to keep all of their digital communications organized without even spending several hours doing it themselves.

Applying smart assistants such as Findo and Yva, employees can easily automate their mailboxes, and track and characterize the data by using very contextual reference points as well as metadata, opening up the probability of finding different opportunities that would go unnoticed otherwise.

BrionScheidel says, in this process, the key capability is the categorization which is done through text analytics of customer experience platform developer MaritzCX. Firstly, by defining a set of categories and after that assigning the text to them, the first step can be taken by the organization in the direction of removing the clutter from the unstructured data and further putting it into a useable and quantifiable form.

At the moment, there are two main methodologies which are rules-based and machine learning, both of which have their own good points as well as bad points. A clearer definition of the hope that the people hope to achieve and the way of doing so can be provided by a rule-based approach, while the ML provides a more intuitive means of adjusting to the changing conditions, even though, not always in ways which produce optimum results. Today in this time, the MaritzCX depends exclusively on rules-based analysis.

However, just as the technology makes it possible to deal with one interactable problem, in this time-honored tradition, probably there can be much greater complexity in it. In such case, the open-source community is there which has started looking at the past mere infrastructure and applications to the actual data.

A new open – data framework known as the Community Data License that is CDLA was announced by the Linux Foundation. This framework is intended to provide a wider access to the data which will otherwise be restricted for some specific users.

In such a way, the data-based collaborative communities become able to share the knowledge across Hadoop, Spark, and some other Big Data Platform, furthermore, adding more sources of the unstructured information that should be captured, analyzed, and conditioned so as to make it useful. Nowadays, the same techniques are being deployed in-house that is likely to be able, in order to handle these new volumes. But the CDLA has the potential to significantly increase the challenge which is still intoxicating.

The key determinant of success in the digital economy will likely be the proper conditioning of unstructured data. In today's scenario, those who have the most advanced and upgraded infrastructure can generally leverage their might in order to keep the competitors at bay.

Despite all this, the constant democratization of the infrastructure by using the cloud and service level architectures is rapidly leveling the playing field. Moving ahead, the winner will not be the one who has the most resources or even most of the data, it will be the one who has the ability to act upon actual knowledge.

1.7. CASE STUDY: GERMAN TELECOM COMPANY

1.7.1. Digital Transformation Enables Telecom to Provide Customer Touch Points with an Improved Experience

Digital-based technologies and approaches have already had a huge impact on the telecom industry and the services delivered to customers, with further, more rapid changes expected. "Customers are increasingly become tech-savvy and expect faster, simpler services to be delivered through the digital medium," said the Director of IT from one of the largest telecom organizations in Germany.

On one hand, the use of digital technologies can help improve customer understanding and retention, but on the other, it can increase the competitiveness within the market and contribute to rapidly changing customer needs.

The company attributes its position and success in placing customer needs at the heart of its business. A range of digital-based approaches are used, not just to better understand customers' current needs, but to help the company better anticipate their future demands.

Examples of this include adopting an omni-channel approach to service delivery and investing in big data analytics to drive deep customer understanding. Developing deep customer insight and predictive models have required the adoption of new tools such as big data analytics, CRM, online customer experience management, cloud expense management and managed mobility services. It has also required a change in mind-set to help envision the future so the right investments can be made.

"We have deployed big data technology to get insight into our customers, improve the experience of our customers at different touch points, as well as ensure quick and simple rollouts of products and services," he said. Furthermore, digital-based strategies are increasingly being used to build relationships with end customers as well as provide platforms for marketing and sales activities.

Examples of these include online customer care portals, an expanded social media presence and using various digital channels to execute sales and marketing objectives. Digital transformation is also having an impact on internal processes. Partnerships with vendors of digital process management and CRM systems have enabled the company to quickly create new products and services in the most cost effective manner.

"Utilizing digital technology to better serve our customers has transformed the way our organization operates," he explained. Increasing digitization brings with it increasing security risks, both for data protection and for uninterrupted service delivery. One example is the rapid growth in mobile payment services, requiring robust security regardless of the device used.

To counter this, the company has undertaken a comprehensive approach to implement security in accordance with global standards and conducts a battery of tests to continually improve. Given the increased sensitivity, risk, and potential damage of a cyber-attack, cyber security remains an investment priority for the company. Digital transformation will continue to have a significant impact on the telecommunications industry.

As new technologies and advancements enter the market, the company will face new complications and obstacles. To counter this, the company will continue to develop new counter mechanisms and solutions to respond to these obstacles and create a disruption of their own. Strategic partners are a vital aspect of digital transformation and future obstacles cannot be overcome without their assistance. "In the next five years we will develop more partnerships so that we can utilize technologies that help us understand our customers better, resulting in major cost savings, and assist us in management of operations in multiple locations," he concluded.

1.8. CHECKPOINTS

1. Define data and Big Data.
2. Enumerate the various characteristics of Big Data.
3. How are computer systems used for processing Big Data differ from normal computers?
4. Define the following terms with respect to Big Data:
   i) Volume;
   ii) Velocity; and
   iii) Variety.
5. Explain the term 'Analytics.'
6. With the help of the diagram, illustrate the Web Analytics Process.
7. What are the different kinds of Analytics that are used for Big Data Analysis?
8. Explain the term 'Veracity' with respect to Big Data systems.
9. Define the term 'Unstructured Data' and 'Structured Data.'
10. Why is unstructured data considered as qualitative data?

CHAPTER 2

Identifier Systems

LEARNING OBJECTIVE

In this chapter, you will learn about:

- The meaning of identifier systems;
- The various features of identifier systems;
- The identifiers in database;
- The various classes of identifiers;
- The processes and techniques in de-identification; and
- Risk assessment of re-identification.

Keywords

Identifier System, One-way Hash function, Immutability, Reconciliation, Autonomy, De-identification, Pseudonymization, K-anonymization, Re-Identification, Regular Identifiers, Database Identifiers

2.1. MEANING OF IDENTIFIER SYSTEM

An object identifier is an alphanumeric string. For many Big Data resources, human beings are the greatest concern for the data managers. This is because, many Big Data resources are developed to store and retrieve information about individuals. Another factor that makes a data manager more concerned about human identifiers is that it is extremely important to establish human identity with absolute certainty. This is required for blood transfusion and banking transactions.

Identifiers	
Symbol	miR-206
Alt. Symbols	MIR206
miRBase	MI0000490
miRBase family	MIPF0000038
Entrez	406989
HUGO	31584
OMIM	611599
Ensembl	ENSG00000207604

2.2. FEATURES OF AN IDENTIFIER SYSTEM

These are very strong reasons to store all information that is present within data objects. As a result, the most important task for data managers is creating a dependable identifier system. The features of a good identifier system are as follows:

2.2.1. Completeness

This means that all unique objects in Big Data resource must have an identifier.

2.2.2. Uniqueness

All identifiers must maintain a unique sequence.

2.2.3. Exclusivity

Each identifier is assigned to a unique object which is not assigned to any other object.

2.2.4. Authenticity

The objects that receive identification must be verified as the objects that are intended to be. For example, if an individual walks into a bank and claims that he is Mr. X, the bank has to ensure that he actually is who he claims to be.

2.2.5. Aggregation

The Big Data resource must be capable of accumulating all data that is associated with the identifier. In case of a bank, this would imply that it has to collect all transactions linked to the account. A hospital is concerned with collecting all data associated with the patients' identifiers like clinic visit records, lab test results, medication transactions. In order for the identifier system to function properly, aggregation methods have to collect all the data associated with an object.

2.2.6. Permanence

The identifiers and their data have to be maintained permanently. For example, in a hospital system, if a patient returns after 20 years, the recorders should be able to access the identifier and gather all information related to the patient. Even if the patient dies, his identifier must not be lost.

2.2.7. Reconciliation

A mechanism is required for reconciliation which can facilitate the merger of data associated with a unique identified object in one Big Data resource with data held in another resource for the same object. Reconciliation is a process that requires authentication, merging, and comparison. A good example is a reconciliation found in health record portability. When a patient visits a hospital, the hospital may have to gather her records from her previous hospital. Both the hospitals have to ensure that the patient has been identified correctly and combine the records.

2.2.8. Immutability

The identifier should never be destroyed or lost and should remain unchanged. In the event of the following, one data object is assigned to two identifiers belonging to both the merging system:

- In case two Big Data resources are merged;
- In case the legacy data is merged into a Big Data resources; and
- In case individual data objects from two different Big Data resources are merged.

In the above cases, the identifiers must be preserved without making changes to them. The merged data object must be provided with annotative information specifying the origin of each identifier. In other words, it must be explained which identifier has come from which Big Data resource.

2.2.9. Security

The identifier system is at risk of malicious attacks. There is a chance that a Big Data resource with an identifier system can be corrupted irreversibly. The identifier system is particularly vulnerable when the identifiers have been modified. In the case of a human-based identifier system, identifiers may be stolen with the purpose of causing harm to the individual whose records are a part of the resource.

2.2.10. Documentation and Quality Assurance

An identifier system should be there to find and rectify errors in the patient identifier system. There must be protocols in place which can establish identifier systems, safeguard the system, assigning identifiers and for monitoring the system. All the issues and corrective action should be recorded and reviewed.

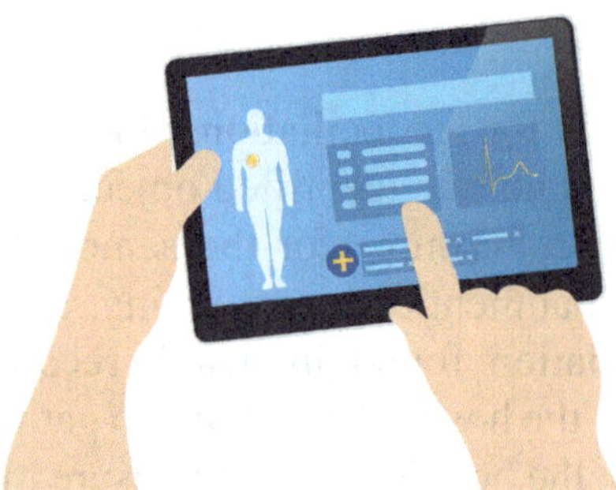

The review procedure is important because it can indicate whether the errors were corrected effectively and whether any measures are required to improve the identifier system. Everything should be documented, be it procedures, actions or any modification to the system. This is a complex job.

2.2.11. Centrality

An identifier system plays a central role in all kinds of information system whether it belongs to a savings bank, a prison, hospital, or airline. Information systems can be perceived as a scaffold of identifiers to which data is attached. For example, in case of a hospital information system, the patient identifier is most vital as every patient transaction is attached to it.

2.2.12. Autonomy

An identifier system has an independent existence. It is independent of the data contained in Big Data Resources. The identifiers system can persist, organize, and document the present and future data objects even if all data contained in the Big Data disappear. This could happen if they are deleted inadvertently.

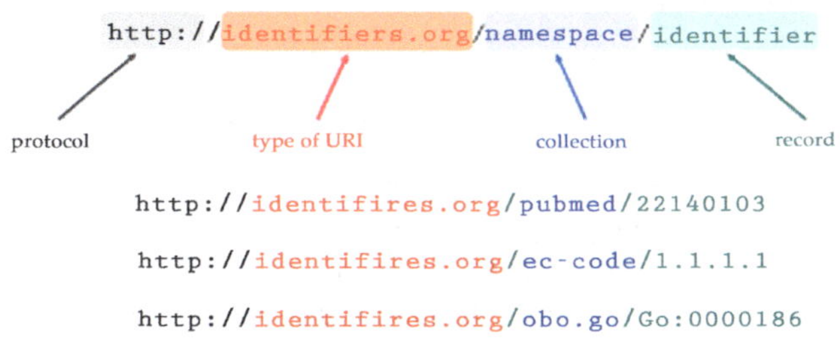

Example of Identification in Jazz Songs from the 1930's

Data identification project will create spreadsheets of word frequencies found in jazz songs from the 1930's. For each song a plain text document containing a transcript of the lyrics will be generated and stored as a .txt file. Word counts for each song analyzed will be recorded in spreadsheets, one for each song. Another spreadsheet will contain the details about each of the songs that were analyzed (such as year written, singer, producer, etc.). A final spreadsheet will combine the word counts from all of the songs analyzed. The spreadsheets will be saved as both Microsoft Excel and .csv files.

2.3. DATABASE IDENTIFIERS

The name database object is referred to as its identifier. Databases, servers, and database objects, like the tables, columns, views, indexes, constraints, procedures, and rules, can have identifiers. Identifiers are needed for most objects but are optional for some of the objects like constraints.

An object identifier is formed when the object is defined. Then, the identifier is used in order to reference the object.

The collation of an identifier relies on the level at which it is defined. Identifiers of instance-level objects, like logins and database names, are allocated the default collation of the instance. Identifiers of objects in a database, like the tables, and column names, and views are assigned the default collation of the database.

For instance, two tables with names that vary only in case can be formed in a database that has case-sensitive collation. On the other hand, it cannot be formed in a database that has case-insensitive collation.

2.4. CLASSES OF IDENTIFIERS

There are two classes of identifiers.

Regular Identifiers	Follow the rules for the format of identifiers. When the regular identifiers are used in Transact-SQL statements, they are not delimited
Delimited Identifiers	These types of identifiers are written inside double quotation marks (") or brackets ([]). Identifiers that follow the rules for the format of identifiers might not be delimited.

On the other hand, identifiers that do not follow all the rules for identifiers must be delimited in a Transact-SQL statement.

Both regular as well as delimited identifiers must comprise 1 to 128 characters. In the case of local temporary tables, the identifier can have a maximum of 116 characters.

2.5. RULES FOR REGULAR IDENTIFIERS

Learning Activity
Using Identifiers
Find ways in which the usage of identifiers can provide value to a dataset that has data on the identification numbers of the residents of a city in the state of Illinois, USA.

The names of variables, functions, and stored procedures must follow the following rules for Transact-SQL identifiers.

1. The first character must be one of the following:

- A letter as defined by the Unicode Standard 3.2. The Unicode definition of letters comprises Latin characters from a to z, from A to Z, and also letter characters from other languages.
- The underscore (_), at sign (@), or number sign (#).

Certain symbols in the starting of an identifier have special meaning in SQL Server. A regular identifier that begins with the at sign always represents a local variable or parameter. This identifier cannot be used as the name of any other kind of object.

On the other hand, an identifier that begins with a number sign represents a temporary table or procedure. Also, an identifier that begins with double number signs (##) represents a global temporary object. Although the number sign or double number sign characters can be used to start the names of other kinds of objects.

Some Transact-SQL functions have names that begin with double at signs (@@). In order to avoid confusion with these functions, one should not make use of the names that begin with @@.

2. Subsequent characters can consist of the following:

- Letters as defined in the Unicode Standard 3.2.
- Decimal numbers from either Basic Latin or other national scripts.
- The at sign, dollar sign ($), number sign, or underscore.

3. The identifier must not be a Transact-SQL reserved word. SQL Server reserves both the uppercase as well as lowercase versions of reserved words. When identifiers are used in Transact-SQL statements, the identifiers that do not follow these rules must be delimited by double quotation marks or brackets.

The words that are reserved rely on the compatibility level of the database.

This level can be set by the use of the ALTER DATABASE statement.

4. Embedded spaces or special characters cannot be used.
5. Supplementary characters are not used.

2.6. ONE-WAY HASH FUNCTION

The one-way hash function can also be referred to as the message digest, fingerprint or compression function. It is a mathematical function that takes a variable-length input string and thus, converts it into a fixed-length binary sequence. In addition to this, a one-way hash function is designed in such a way that it becomes hard to reverse the process which means that in order to find a string which hashes to a given value and therefore, it is referred to as one-way. A good hash function also makes it difficult to find the two strings which would produce the same hash value.

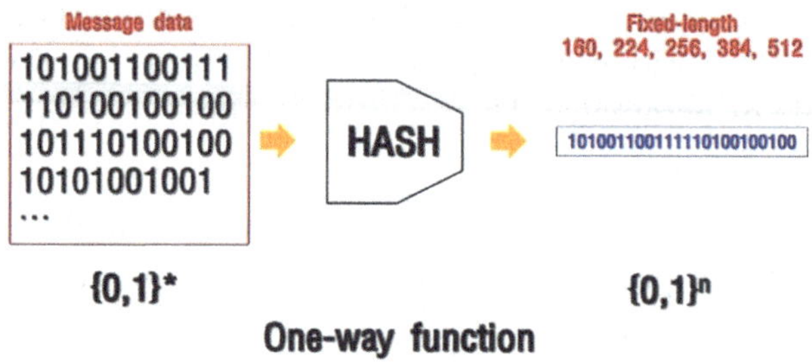

All the modern hash algorithms produce a hash value of 128 bits and also greater than that.

If in case, there is a small change in an input string then that should cause the hash value to change drastically. Even if 1 bit is flipped in the input string, then as a result, minimum half of the bits in the hash value will flip. This is referred to as the avalanche effect.

A document's hash can serve as a cryptogenic equivalent of the document because of the fact that it is computationally infeasible to produce a document that would hash to a given value or find both the two documents which hash to the same value. In such a way, it can make one-way hash function as a central notion in public-key cryptography.

While producing a digital signature for any document, it is no longer needed to encrypt the whole document with a sender's private key which in case, can be extremely slow. It is enough to encrypt the hash value of the document instead of doing all the things.

Despite the fact that, a one-way hash function is used mostly in order to generate digital signatures, it can have other practical applications as well as the secure password storage, file identification and message authentication code.

One-way hash functions can be used in order to transform the input messages of various lengths into the output sequences of a fixed length that are usually shorter. The output sequence is often referred to as hash value. In most of the cases, the hash values are used to mark the input sequences, which means to assign to them the unique values which can characterize them.

It is easy to compute their value which is based on the input data but having only a hash value one cannot further determine the original input sequence. A one-way hash function needs to be a collision-free.

There are certain algorithms of the one-way hash function which is often known to the public. They provide security because of the properties as one-way functions. The data is generated by the hash function which should be pseudorandom.

One-way hash functions are used in order to protect the data against intentional or unintentional alterations. Having some data, one can calculate or estimate a checksum that may be attached to the message and checked by other recipients (by calculating the same checksum and compare it with the checksum value that is received). For instance, they are used in a message authentication algorithm HMAC.

In addition to it, hash functions are used for the purpose of storing data in an effective manner, in so-called hash tables. Data can be accessed by finding the hash values. Hash values are stored in the memory of the computer.

2.6.1. Hash Function Expanding

Having a hash function that functions on small blocks of data, one can expand this function and make a new function. This new function will operate on larger input data of several sizes. Is such a way, it is possible to calculate a hash value for any messages. In order to attain this, one can make use of so-called Merkle-Damgard construction.

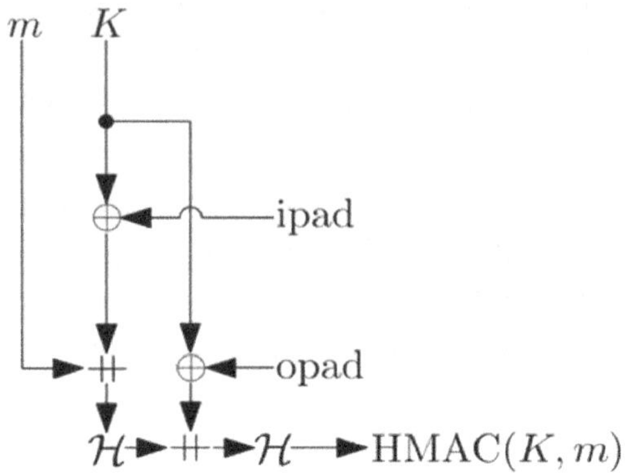

A scheme that is mentioned below presents a way of using multiple hash functions (h: T x X -> T, where T is a set of all possible hash values) that permits to calculate a hash value for the whole message (H: X^L -> T). Every single hash function operates on one data block.

2.6.2. Hash Algorithms

The Microsoft cryptographic providers support these hash algorithms: MD4, MD5, SHA, and SHA256.

MD4 & MD5

Ron Rivest invented MD4 as well as MD5. MD stands for Message Digest. Both algorithms generate 128-bit hash values. MD5 is considered as an enhanced version of MD4.

SHA

SHA stands for Secure Hash Algorithm. It was designed by NIST and NSA. SHA generates 160-bit hash values. The hash value is longer as compared to that of MD4 and MD5. SHA is generally considered safer as compared to the other algorithms and is the recommended hash algorithm.

SHA256

SHA256 is a 256-bit modern version of SHA. SHA256 is only supported by the Microsoft Enhanced RSA and AES Cryptographic Provider.

2.7. DE-IDENTIFICATION AND DATA SCRUBBING

De-identification refers to the process which is used to prevent an individual's personal identity from getting revealed. This is an important aspect of data privacy. Another important concept discussed here is Data Scrubbing. The term data scrubbing refers to the process of amending or removing incorrect, duplicated, incomplete or incorrectly formatted data. The following are explained in detail hereafter:

- Concept of De-identification;
- The process of De-identification;
- Techniques of De-identification;
- Assessing the Risk of Re-Identification;
- Data Scrubbing;
- Meaning of Bad Data; and
- Approaches to Improve Data Quality.

2.8. CONCEPT OF DE-IDENTIFICATION

The process of data de-identification refers to the removal of all data that indicate personally sensitive information. A major data security and compliance concern for all organizations are protecting Personally Identifiable Information and Protected Health Information.

De-identification is not an exact science, rather a risk management exercise. Hence it can be called a contentious contemporary issue. Some experts argue that digital information capabilities have become so advanced that it can never be truly identified.

If organizations require complex de-identification exercises like when information is sensitive or the de-identified data has to be shared with the public, the services of a specialist expert is generally used.

2.8.1. Purpose of De-Identification

The main aim of de-identification is to allow data to be used by others without revealing the identity or too much personal information of the individuals to whom the data pertains. It is generally used to:

- Safeguard the privacy of individuals and organizations.
- Ensure that the whereabouts of valuable things like archaeological

findings or scarce minerals or threatened animal species are not revealed to the public.

2.9. THE PROCESS OF DE-IDENTIFICATIONS

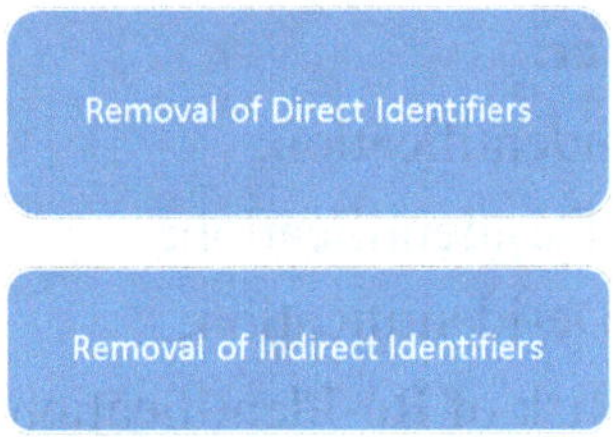

The data de-identification process involves:

- Removal of direct identifiers

In order to de-identify data, some direct identifiers like names, addresses, contact information etc. are removed from the data.

- Removal of quasi identifier

One concern is the presence of indirect identifiers. These data elements do not reveal the identity of an individual when used in isolation, but when used in combination with other data, it can identify an individual. Hence, these indirect identifiers should also be considered for removal based on the data collected. Examples of indirect identifiers are occupation, age or ethnicity. Though not always problematic but, it can still identify a person when a certain combination is applied which can restrict the data to a small population. For example, there may be just one Aboriginal man Alton aged between 25 to 30. Appropriate data filters can help in obtaining other personal information about this individual.

The process of de-identification involves time and money. Sometimes, the process of de-identification can render the data valueless. This limitation of the process makes the solution less perfect for sharing sensitive data. Hence each organization has to decide whether it is suitable for the data being collected and the purpose for which it is used. However, it is better than not sharing any data with the public at all.

Learning Activity
De-Identifying the Data
Find the implications if the data of people used by social media platforms is not de-identified and reflect upon the consequences that such a failure can lead to.

2.10. TECHNIQUES OF DE-IDENTIFICATION

The common techniques used for de-identification are:

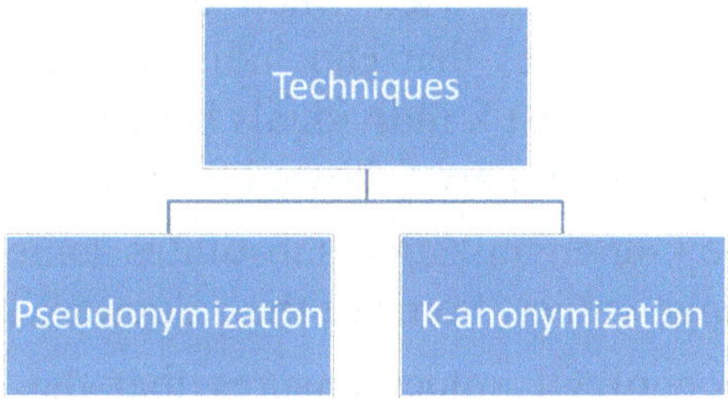

- Pseudonymization: It is used to mask personal identifiers from records; and
- K-anonymization: It is used to generalize quasi-identifiers.

2.10.1. Pseudonymization

This process involves the replacement of all identifying attributes which are unique to another. Examples of such attributes are gender, race, etc. However, the owner of the original data can identify the data directly, referred to as reidentification. For example, if all identifying data elements are eliminated and just an internal numerical identifier is left, a third person will find it impossible to re-identify the data. However, the data owner can re-identify easily. The pseudonymized data still remains personal information.

The pseudonymized data are generally not used as test data. Test data must be anonymized. One can depend on randomly generated data from sites that offer such services. Pseudonymization minimizes the possibility of a third person linking the data sets with the original identity of the data subject. Thereby, legal issues pertaining to de-identification and anonymization of personal data is avoided before it is made available in the big data space.

Certain guidelines are followed to implement the pseudonymization technique. This helps in securing data and prevents it from being identifiable at the data-subject level. They are:

- Elimination of the ability to link data sets to other data sets. This makes the identification of anonymized data uniquely identifiable.
- Ensuring secure storage of encryption key and keeping it separately from the encrypted data.
- Use of physical, administrative, and technical security measures to protect data.

2.10.2. K-anonymization

K-anonymization technique is used when dealing with quasi identifier attributes. It defines attributes that can indirectly reveal the individual's identity. It ensures that at least k individuals have the same combination of QI values. Standard guidelines are followed for handling QI values.

For example, the k-anonymization substitutes some original data in the records with new range values. Some of the values are left unchanged.

New combination of QI values ensures that the individuals are not identified. At the same time, the data records are not destroyed.

There are two common methods used for K-anonymization.

- Suppression Method: In this method asterisk "*" is used as a substitute for certain values of the attributes. Some or all values of a column may be replaced using an asterisk.
- Generalization Method: In this method, a wider range of values are used as a substitute for individual values. For example, the attribute 'Age' can be replaced by an age range, like writing 20–25 for the age of 22.

Though k-anonymization has a lot of potential in case of group-based anonymization. This is because it is simple and can perform a wide array of algorithms. It is vulnerable to various threats. These attacks become more effective when the attacker has background knowledge. These attacks include:

Homogeneity Attack: This type of attack happens when all values for a sensitive value contained in a k record are the same. In these cases, though data has been k-anonymized, the sensitive values can be predicted with reasonable accuracy.

Background Knowledge Attack: This attack leverages the linkage between one or more quasi-identifier attributes with the sensitive attribute. For example, the knowledge that low rates of heart attacks are attributed to Japanese patients can be used to narrow down the range of values for a sensitive attribute of a patient's disease.

Example of Re-identification

Researchers from the U.S. and China collaborated on a project to re-identify users in a national de-identified physical activity dataset using machine learning, a type of artificial intelligence. They used data from 14,451 individuals included in the National Health and Nutrition Examination Surveys from 2003–04 and 2005–06, all of which had been stripped of geographic and protected health information. The research team tested whether two different AI algorithms could re-identify the patients in the dataset, both of which were fairly successful, according to study results published in *JAMA* last month. The algorithms identified users by learning daily patterns in step data and matching them to their demographic data. One of the algorithms, for example, was based on a machine learning technique called the random forest method. This algorithm accurately matched physical activity data and demographic information to 95% of adults in the 2003–04 dataset and 94% of adults in the 2005–06 dataset.

Various k-anonymity algorithms have been proposed; however, experts believe that the privacy parameter k of k-anonymity has to be known before the algorithm is applied.

2.11. ASSESSING THE RISK OF RE-IDENTIFICATION

An important consideration before releasing the de-identified datasets, is to assess whether the selected techniques and controls implemented in the environment in which the data will be shared has the capacity to manage the risk of re-identification.

Experts believe that in most cases, where a de-dentification process has been performed, it cannot be guaranteed that the risk of re-identification has been totally eliminated. Privacy does not necessitate that de-identification should be absolute. Privacy will be considered adequate and information will be considered de-identified when the risk of the identity of an individual being revealed is very low.

2.11.1. Factors Contributing to Re-identification

Re-identification generally happens because of the following reasons:

- Poor de-identification: This happens when a piece of identifying information is left in the records inadvertently.
- Data linkage: Re-identification may be possible if the de-identified information can be linked with an auxiliary dataset which has the identifying information.
- Pseudonym reversal: If a pseudonym is assigned using an algorithm with a key, it will enable the reversal of the pseudonymization process using the key. This will compromise the identity of the individuals.
- Inferential disclosure: This is possible when personal information can be inferred with reasonable certainty from the statistical attributes of the information.

2.11.2. Risks Assessment of Re-identification

Various factors have to be considered for assessing the risk of re-identification including:

- The structure, content, and value of the original information;
- The nature and robustness of the de-identification technique applied;
- Availability of supplementary information that can be linked with the de-identified information; and
- The resource and the capability of the attacker.

A motivated intruder test is applied to assess whether a reasonably competent person who does not possess any specialized skill can successfully re-identify the information. This can act as a good indicator of the level of risk. This assessment is generally more effective when a specialist is involved. This is particularly important if a high degree of confidence is required that not a single individual can be reasonably identified.

2.12. CASE STUDY: MASTERCARD: APPLYING SOCIAL MEDIA RESEARCH INSIGHTS FOR BETTER BUSINESS DECISIONS

2.12.1. Objective/Brief

One of the few steadfast companies that committed fully to research by making insights more actionable, and became more strategic, efficient, and successful is MasterCard. In 2011, MasterCard's executive leadership challenged the organization to transform the B2B financial services giant into a more consumer-focused technology company.

To do so, MasterCard created the Conversation Suite – a dynamic, global insight and engagement engine – built and supported by a global team of communications and social experts who monitor, engage in and analyze conversations around the world in real-time, 24/7.

The social listening and analysis of public profile social data serve as a barometer, a resource, and as a foundation for communication decision-making. One demonstration of MasterCard's ability to transform data into insights, actions, and business results, relates to its efforts in mobile payments, an emerging form of commerce-enabled through the use of mobile devices.

MasterCard is a technology company in the global payments industry. They operate the world's fastest payments processing network, connecting consumers, financial institutions, merchants, governments, and businesses in more than 210 countries and territories.

MasterCard's products and solutions make everyday commerce activities – such as shopping, traveling, running a business and managing finances – easy, secure, and efficient In 2011, the mobile phone became the consumer method of choice for making purchases and managing money.

MasterCard was perfectly placed to help merchants provide their customers with a safe, simple, smart way to pay using their mobile devices. In a strategic drive, MasterCard led developments of standards and was among the first to launch mobile commerce technologies that let people, "pay with a tap."

As part of this drive, the MasterCard executive team embarked on a journey to transform the B2B financial services giant into a more consumer-focused payments technology company. From a communications standpoint, MasterCard was squarely B2B; the opportunity was to shift engagement online and develop a direct relationship and dialogue with consumers and influencers.

2.12.2. Leading the Mobile Payments Industry Agenda

MasterCard's insights were used as an industry barometer for understanding consumer and merchant adoption. The study revealed significant year-over-year improvements on a number of key performance indicators:

- The 2015 study tracked 2 million global social media posts about mobile payments across social channels up from 85,000 posts in

2012, the first year of the study.

- The sentiment was on the upswing in 2015 with 95% of consumers feeling positive or neutral about mobile payments technology, an increase of 1 percentage point over 2014 and 18 percentage points over 2013.
- Safety & security of mobile payments continues to drive conversations with sentiment improving further in 2015, now 94% positive or neutral, a 3 percentage point increase over the 2014 study. This reflects an overall trend across all years of the study, where security sentiment was 77% positive or neutral in 2013 and 70% in 2012.

The 2015 study was revealed at the Mobile World Congress where MasterCard was at the center of all mobile payment conversations throughout one of the industry's most important events. Striking data visualization assisted in the spread of the story and intensive media interest. The data insights were covered extensively throughout global mainstream and social media.

2.12.3. Results

In a world where many global organizations sit in limbo debating social media's impact on Big Data decision-making, MasterCard committed fully to research, applied the findings, and became more strategic, efficient, and successful. The company's data and insights aid in the execution of communications campaigns in real-time – whether identifying and responding to an issue or facilitating creative opportunities to position the brand with media, influencers, and consumers.

Over the course of the last four years, MasterCard's social insights have been used to successfully inform communications strategy, shape product messaging, and facilitate successful targeting. MasterCard has effectively shifted consumer conversations from questioning available mobile options and the security of mobile, to the possibilities of enhanced experiences through tech innovations on digital devices.

A 40-foot screen located in the atrium in the heart of MasterCard's corporate office, the physical Conversation Suite has become a coveted destination for MasterCard employees, heightening awareness of the importance of the millions of online conversations shaping the brand and industry and serving as a flexible space for brainstorming and information sharing.

The Conversation Suite has helped to evolve the company culture to be more open and collaborative, by demonstrating best-in-class engagement within the industry and transforming MasterCard into a more consumer-focused, aware, and insights-led technology payments company.

Throughout the four years of its Mobile Payments study, MasterCard's traditional market research study confirmed the integrity of the social media insights, delivered in a fraction of the time and at a significantly lower relative cost. MasterCard's social media analysis now works to complement MasterCard's surveys as data-integration adds context and rigor to the findings.

The Conversation Suite has helped evolve the MasterCard culture to be more open and collaborative, demonstrate best-in-class engagement within the industry, and meet the challenge of transforming MasterCard into a more consumer-focused, aware, and insights-led technology. payments company.

2.13. CHECKPOINTS

1. Define the term 'Identifier System.'
2. Explain the features of the Identifier System.
3. What are the different classes of Identifiers Systems?
4. What are Database Identifiers?
5. What are the various rules for using regular identifiers?
6. Explain the one-way hash function.
7. What is meant by 'de-identification'?
8. What is the main concept of de-identification of data?
9. Explain the techniques of data de-identification.
10. What are the risks associated with data re-identification of data?

CHAPTER 3

Improving the Quality of Big Data and Its Measurement

LEARNING OBJECTIVE

In this chapter, you will learn about:

- The process of data scrubbing;
- The improvement of data quality;
- Sentiment analysis and network analysis;
- The ways of measuring the ROI in Big Data;
- Balancing the hard and soft benefits;
- The relevance of real world and real time ROI

Keywords

Data Scrubbing, Bad Data, Sentiment Analysis, Network Analysis, Big Data ROI, Hard, and Soft benefits, Real Time ROI, Data Quality

3.1. DATA SCRUBBING

The era of "Big Data" is characterized by both good and bad data. Data hygiene and data quality are integral to the overall success of any organization.

The term data scrubbing refers to the process of amending or removing incorrect, duplicated, incomplete or incorrectly formatted data. The act of data scrubbing is an early step. It is performed before the data is transferred to the subsequent steps such as data warehousing.

Through the term data scrubbing and data cleaning are used interchangeably but they do not denote the same. Data cleaning is a simpler process that involves the removal of inconsistencies. Whereas, data scrubbing includes specialized steps like decoding, filtering, merging, and translating.

3.2. MEANING OF BAD DATA

Bad data are basically those that are:

- Incorrect;
- Obsolete;
- Redundant;
- Improperly formatted; and
- Incomplete.

The goal of data scrubbing is not just limited to cleaning up data in a database. It also aims to make data sets that have been merged from different databases consistent. Organizations generally use sophisticated software applications to clean up the data. These software use algorithms, look-up tables, rules, and other tools. This task was once done humanly and hence prone to human errors.

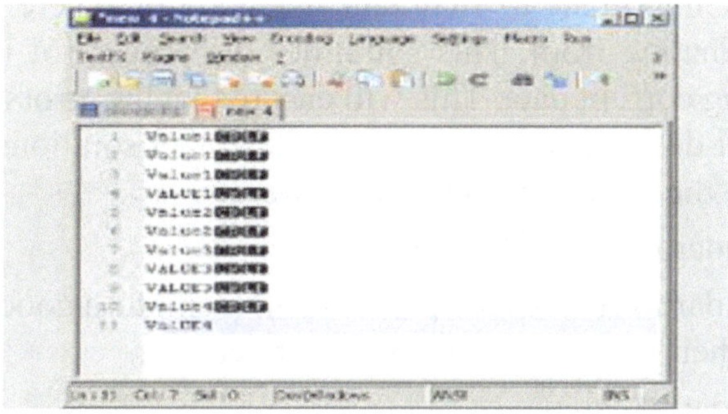

3.2.1. Cost Implications of Bad Data

As per the Data Warehousing Institute, bad data costs US businesses more than $500 billion every year. As per an estimate, a typical business loses almost 12% of net income from the bottom line due to insufficient data hygiene. In other words, a business can improve the bottom line by at least 10% if it maintains data hygiene.

Example of Enron Scandal as Bad Data

During the early 2000s Enron grew to be the sixth-largest energy company in the world with soarings to ckprices throughout the late 1990s and early 2000s. However, a host of fraudulent financial data led to their eventual collapse in 2001. It turns out that the data being provided to shareholders in annual reports and financial statements were largely fictionalized. Dozens of indictments resulted in many Enron executives being in carcerated.

3.3. COMMON APPROACHES TO IMPROVE DATA QUALITY

As per a report, only 30% of the organizations have a data quality strategy in place. The other 70 address these data quality problems only when they appear. They generally pursue simple cures like manual checking otherwise. Irrespective of whether a business has an appropriate data quality strategy in place or not, ideally it should look for cost-effective ways to improve data hymenia.

3.3.1. Data Scrubbing Steps

Some of the best practices that are involved in data scrubbing process are:

- Monitor Errors

  It is important to maintain a record of where the errors are originating from. This simplifies the process of identifying and fixing corrupt data. This will ensure that the errors do not clog up other departments, especially when other solutions are integrated with the fleet management software.

- Standardize Your Processes

  Standardization of the process will facilitate a good point of entry. Further, it reduces the risk of duplication.

- Validate Accuracy

  Post cleansing the database, the accuracy of the data has to be validated. The appropriate data tools have to be selected that can facilitate the real-time cleanup of data. Some of the tools are equipped with machine learning which makes it efficient for testing accuracy.

- Scrub for Duplicate Data

  It is important to identify duplicates since it will save time while analysing data. In order to avoid duplicity, different data cleaning tools which can analyse raw data in bulk and also automate the entire process.

- Analyse

  The next step would be to append the data using a third party source. A reliable third-party source can capture information from the owner directly, clean, and compile the data. This provides a piece of more complete information that facilitates business intelligence (BI) and analytics.

- Communicate with the Team

  The most important step is to communicate the standardized cleaning process to the team. After scrubbing the data, it has to be cleaned. This will facilitate the development and strengthening of consumer segmentation and share more targeted information with them.

3.4. MEASURING BIG DATA

Data itself is quite often inconsequential in its own right. Measuring or calculating the value of data is considered as a boundless process which consists of endless options and approaches, whether it is structured or unstructured, data is only as valuable as the business results it makes possible.

It is how the users make use of data that permits them to completely understand its true value and potential to enhance the decision-making capabilities. From a business stand point, calculate it against the outcome of positive business outcomes.

There are several approaches that helps in improving the process of decision making of the business and to determine the ultimate value of data, which consists of data warehouses, BI systems, and analytics sandboxes and solutions.

These approaches focus on the significance of every individual data item that goes into these systems. And as a result of this, it highlights the significance of every single outcome linking to business impacts delivered.

The characteristics of big data are defined popularly through the four Vs: volume, velocity, variety, and veracity, as has been discussed before. The adaptation of these four characteristics provides multiple dimensions to the value of data at hand.

Fundamentally, there is a supposition that the data has great potential, but no one has explored where that might be. Unlike a BI system, where analysts are aware of the information they are searching for, the possibilities of discovering big data are all connected to recognize the connections among things they are not aware of. It is all about designing the system in order to decipher or decrypt this information.

A possible approach could be to take the four Vs into prime consideration and determine what kind of value they deliver while resolving a particular problem of the business.

3.4.1. Volume-Based Value

In present times, the organizations have the capability to store as much data as possible in a cost-effective way. In addition to it, they also have the capabilities to do broader examination across different data dimensions and deeper analysis going back to several years of the past context behind data.

In essence, they no longer need to do a sampling of data. They can carry out their analysis or examination on the complete data set. The scenario applies to require into developing true customer-centric profiles, as well as richer customer-centric offerings at a micro-level.

The more amount of data that the businesses have on the customers, both recent as well as historical, the greater the insights. In turn, this will lead to creating better decisions around acquiring, retaining, increasing, and handling those customer relationships.

3.4.2. Velocity-Based Value

This is all about speed. In present times, speed is more important than ever. The faster the businesses can insert the data into their data and analytics platform, the more time will be spent in asking about the right or appropriate questions and seeking answers. The quick analysis capabilities provide businesses with the right decision in time in order to attain their customer relationship management (CRM) objectives.

3.4.3. Variety-Based Value

In this age of digital era, having the capability so as to acquire and analyse various data is extremely valuable. This is because the businesses have the most diverse customer data and so, they can develop a more multi-faceted view about their customers.

This will develop deep insights into the successfully developed and personalized customer journey maps and furthermore, also provides a platform so that the businesses can become more engaged and aware of the customer needs and expectations.

3.4.4. Veracity-Based Value

While there are many questions arising on the quality and accuracy of the data in the context of big data, but in the case of innovative business offerings the accuracy of data is not much critical, at least in the early stages of the concept design and validations. Thus, the more business hypotheses can be churned out from this large amount of the data and it should have greater potential for the business differentiation edge.

While considering these aspects, the development of the framework of measurement allows the businesses to easily measure the value of the data in their most important metric – money.

Once, a big data analytics platform is implemented and it measures along the four V's which the businesses can utilize and further extend the outcomes in order to directly affect the customer acquisition, on boarding, retention, up sell, cross-sell ad other revenue generating indicators.

This can further result in measuring the value of the parallel improvements in operational productivity and the influence of data across the enterprise for such other initiatives.

On the other hand of the spectrum, it is important to note that arranging a lot of data does not necessarily deliver the insights. Nowadays, businesses have access to more data than ever. Despite this, having access to ore data can make it harder to distill the insights. This is because the bigger the datasets, the harder it becomes to search, visualize, and analyse.

The amount of the data is not a subject of matter, but it is how smartly the organizations are dealing with the data that they have. In reality, they can have a lot of data to deal with, but they are not using it in an intelligent way and so, it rarely delivers what they are looking for.

Learning Activity

The Cleaning of Data

Try to enlist some examples of the companies related to keeping bank account records of the customers in which the data scrubbing or cleaning can help in significant ways. What, do you think can be the advantage of cleaning data in such cases?

3.5. HOW TO MEASURE BIG DATA

Analysis of the big data can help in public diplomats' gauge online sentiment and reaction to initiatives, along with the identification of public influencers.

3.5.1. Sentiment Analysis

Definition: The process of deriving emotion and opinion from a data set is referred to as sentiment analysis.

Purpose: This process helps diplomats in order to understand how initiatives, policies, and posts are received by the target audience. This analysis contains a number of benefits for public diplomats who hope to convert large data sets into comprehensible and useful information.

Working:

- Computational Natural Language Processing (NLP) uses algorithms in order to understand and process the human language.
- It uses keywords such as love, wonderful, best vs. worst, stupid, and waste so as to code tweets as positive, negative, or neutral.
- These programs also consider the familiarity to words which negate sentiment, like aren't isn't, and not.

For example, Cyber-Activists in Iran

- There was a London-based group of researchers who used sentiment analysis following the 2003 Iranian Presidential elections in order to make sense of all of the user-generated input on Twitter, Google+, and Blogs.
- They found that the Iranian Administration had vastly overestimated the support for former President Ahmadinejad.
- This is an example of big data which is providing direct access to the people, rather than having the opinions of the public which was filtered through an Administration that can have a motive to misrepresent. The ability to accurately ascertain public sentiment can help the US create a more effective foreign policy.

3.5.2. Network Analysis

Definition: This analysis is a mathematical analysis which helps in visualizing relationships between interacting units.

Purpose: Network analysis provides a visual representation of vast amounts of data points which would otherwise be too difficult to understand. Network maps show diplomats and MFAs who are interacting with their content the most, identify groups that discuss relevant issues, and reveal local influencers.

Working:

- Network maps are generally made by drawing lines in between interacting units that create a visual representation of a network.
- On Twitter, an interaction contains a retweet, a like, or a reply. Dependence of the thickness of the line is on the number of interactions.
- Network analysis can be done for specific people (President Trump, Pope Francis), or on particular communities or hashtags.

For example, Polarization in Egypt

- During the 2011 crisis, network maps of the Egyptian population showed that the electorate was very polarized.
- Understanding the dynamics on social media allows the US to craft policy which better achieves its goals by implementing foreign public opinion. Ideally, listening to social media users can also help policymakers in order to predict the way the events can play out in the future.

3.6. MEASURING BIG DATA ROI: A SIGN OF DATA MATURITY

The big data ROI is considered as a mark of maturity on the journey of big data for any company. This can happen when the big data projects morph from one-offs which are meant to satisfy a single business unit into something which is much larger.

The small big data project victories are notices as well as they are profitable. Visionary company leaders start to conclude the way big data can transform other business units or even their whole company. Along with the growth of the increasing investments, the big data ROI conversations and calculations start to happen.

Example of good ROI by Sprint and Anonymous

Sprint spoke about using big data analytics to improve quality and customer experience while reducing network errorrates and customer churn. They handle 10s of billions of transactions per day for 53 million users, and their big data analytics put-real-time intelligence into the network, driving a 90% increase in capacity. Similarly, EMC data scientists looked at 5 billion cell user CDR signals per day to save tens of millions of dollars with analytics. The project helped identify service issues and avoidneedless, costly repair work.

3.7. THE INTERPLAY OF HARD AND SOFT BENEFITS

ROI calculations can typically be described the hard benefits such as profits, sales or savings. It is required to see financial benefits from any project that is onboard. However, those hard benefits can be realized, it should also consider the role of soft benefits, the non-financial or intangible benefits which are derived from the ROI journey.

Learning Activity

The ROI in Big Data

Go through the various benefits that can be provided by Big Data in the marketing sector of a healthcare product, and understand the extent to which the ROI on using Big Data can be maximized.

While considering the big data ROI, the skills gained by the team from the early projects are likely to be the first returns that are realized. On the way to data maturity, gaining skills is a measure that a company should take seriously. Without seeing the scenario or use case, having the skills so as to master the big data tasks is a major step towards enabling the future ROI measures.

When the knowledge is received, then the internal team of the company becomes experienced enough to take on the data initiatives and furthermore, run them themselves or in partnership with the external resources. This promotes internal productivity, which eventually fuels the big data projects which can deliver the hard ROI's that is what the company's looking for.

3.8. WHEN BIG DATA PROJECTS REQUIRE BIG INVESTMENTS

Generally, the small-scale big data projects are started by almost all normal companies. The less initial expenses and deliver the fast return of investment are given by these projects. For example, an organization that is less on the data maturity scale might put money in Apache Hadoop or another big data infrastructure that makes the storing of large data sets easy or their enterprise data warehouse increasingly well-organized. The storage ability and the efficiencies over the other storage options have less advantage in comparison to storage ability and the efficiencies that make the return on investment almost immediate.

Though, with the company developing along the data maturity scale, it generally leads to projects that pay attention to analytics, data mining, or real-time data decisions. It needs more of an investment, and estimation of return on investment becomes more difficult.

There is a very fast growth in the number of companies achieving this scale of investment. The yearly New Vantage Partners Big Data Executive Survey in 2017 has stated that 26.8% of the companies surveyed are likely to put money up to the amount of 50 million dollars or more on big data projects. The return of investment efforts becomes very important as the scale of investment reaches millions of dollars.

3.9. REAL-TIME, REAL-WORLD ROI

It has come out in the survey conducted by the New Vantage that the top two reasons organizations invest in big data are to develop increased and deep insights into their business and customers that is 37% and to take benefit of speed quicker time to answer, time to decision, and quicker to market that is 29.7%.

In organizations, there is a target of reaching big data maturity and that is restructuring the internal decision-making culture. The instincts of management executives are not being taken into account any longer as the business decisions will be based on data. The organizations that are progressing towards this culture are more productive and will become profitable in the long run in comparison to competitors that don't take benefit of data-based insights. These are three companies on the road to return on investment:

3.9.1. Streaming Analytics Aim to Optimize Drilling Efforts

The offshore contract-based drilling services are offered by Rowan Companies. In 2019, the law set to come in power that needs real-time safety monitoring. Around the world the fleets are distributed, they require a trustable way to secure this information.

The internet of things (IoT) tags are the basis of the strategy adopted by them. The open-source and analytics platform solutions were executed by Rowan on its first drill-ship in less than ninety days, utilizing 3,200 tags. In the upcoming six months Rowan plans to increase to 25 rigs. The solution will utilize 10,000 tags and a hundred and fifty kilobytes of bandwidth when it is in full operation. The organization can now observe from distance vital conditions. They are supposed to decrease downtime and ease future troubleshooting trips with the use of predictive analytics and maintenance forecasting.

3.9.2. Smarter Energy Reporting Improves Customer Satisfaction

In countries like the UK, Ireland, and North America the power company Centrica provides energy services to 28 million customers. The infrastructure was assessed by them to rethink the ways they might need to grow customer satisfaction that is utilizing the smart meter data. They implemented big data solutions to restructure their evaluation of data. The data aggregation is used by them, and presently they supply correct smart energy reports to customers, giving them increased learning of their electricity use, consumption peaks, and the way their money is being spent. The way Centrica observes energy use is reshaped by the smart metering based totally on data analysis. Data is without difficulty collected, sorted, and analysed each and every 30 minutes for the most reliable and correct reporting.

3.9.3. Connected Data Simplifies Healthcare

There are 35 hospitals and 400 clinics that are run by Mercy that is a U.S. healthcare machine. Their data team made a massive push for one patient, one record utilizing the Epic. It does not matter the way a patient is involved with Mercy; they wanted their up to date patient records in front of clinicians and staff. They wanted to do more advanced analytics that combined Epic facts with external, third-party data sources based on the success of this initiative.

Mercy was in a position to implement a method to do that in real-time by utilizing the open supply platform. There are few researchers employed by a company that was working on a project in their on-campus database platforms. The research team predicted a query runtime of two weeks for a single query that analyzed a patient number of 19,000. Moving that data to the new, Hadoop-based platform, the query took almost half a day to ran.

In each and every company the big data follows the special direction. At the start it is tough to determine the big data return on investment, it is good that it will provide financial benefits in the long run.

3.10. CASE STUDY 2: SOUTHWEST AIRLINES: BIG DATA PR ANALYSIS AIDS ON-TIME PERFORMANCE

3.10.1. Objective/Brief

As one of the top domestic carriers of passengers and their bags in the United States, Southwest Airlines has a 40+ year history as an efficiency machine. For many years, it has held the top spot in the U.S. Department of Transportation Monthly Air Travel Consumer Report as the best on-time domestic airline.

Two years ago, those statistics began to slip, as the airline was working to bring together the schedules of Southwest and its newly acquired subsidiary, AirTran Airways. The airline also pivoted to a more long-haul scheduled airline with more connecting itineraries, all of which created a more complex operating environment.

As a result, Southwest has struggled with on time performance (OTP). It is important to note there is a direct correlation between poor OTP and customer complaints, and a low Net Promoter Score. The business has seen an improvement in OTP recently, a result of new programs and procedures in place to help improve turn times, originator flights, etc., along with diligence and dedication by our Southwest Airlines' employees.

3.10.2. Strategy

An enterprise-wide effort was begun with many moving parts to attempt to improve the airline's operational performance. Initiatives like "Start Strong" were implemented to ensure the first flights of the day left on time, thereby creating a better operational day.

The Communications Team was asked to participate in the enterprise effort and contribute data to a comprehensive view of operation for a holistic view of on-time performance. Then, a cross-functional team would analyze the data to better understand trends with our traveling audience (i.e., complaints, customer service calls, refunds, etc).

3.10.3. Execution/Implementation

Southwest's Ops Recovery Team pulls information monthly from various teams and departments to get a holistic view of how the business is performing when it comes to OTP, specifically in the areas of Operations, Customers, and Finance.

As part of the monthly Ops Recovery Team report, under the Customer umbrella, the communications team would supply data and insight on news coverage and real-time social conversation (sentiment, topics, and volume) that mentioned OTP directly, or, as Customers often reference it: "flight delay," "on time," or "late flight."

3.10.4. Effectiveness of Assignment

The communications data included the number of news and social media mentions daily, daily sentiment, sample of comments, and examples of news coverage, drawing attention to any major news announcement on any given day, like Department of Transportation rankings, or an event that may impact on-time performance, like weather, or ancillary service issue, such as a shutdown of an air traffic control tower.

This data was married with the number of customer complaints that were recorded by the Customer Relations Department, as well as the actual arrival delay in minutes per passenger, to give the team a surgical view of how external factors could be affecting OTP, and helped reiterate that poor OTP will drive an increase in customer calls and inquiries via the telephone and social channels, as well as be directly linked to downturn in the Net Promoter Score.

The business has put several new programs and procedures in place to help combat some of the "cause and effect" results of sluggish on-time performance. Initial results, based on the most recent stats from the Department of Transportation, show Southwest's on-time performance rate for June was 72.5%, or 8th place when compared to other airlines. This was a significant improvement over June 2014, when OTP was 67.6%, and 10th place overall.

3.11. CHECKPOINTS

1. What is meant by data scrubbing?
2. What is Bad Data?
3. What is the need to scrub the 'Bad Data'?
4. Explain sentiment analysis.
5. What is meant by network analysis?
6. Enlist some ways in which data quality can be improved.
7. Explain the four vs. that are taken into consideration while measuring Big Data.
8. What are the scenarios where the Big Data projects require big investments?
9. Enlist some ways in which there has been an improvement in the real time data providing good real time ROI.
10. Explain ways in which benefits can be weighed and measured.

CHAPTER 4

Ontologies

LEARNING OBJECTIVE

In this chapter, you will learn about:

- The meaning of ontologies;
- The main relation of ontologies to Big Data;
- The reason for the development of ontologies;
- The advantages and disadvantages of ontologies;
- The meaning of semantic web; and
- The major components of semantic web.

Keywords
Ontology, Sematic Web, XML, RDF, OWL, P-axis

INTRODUCTION

An ontology is a set of concepts within a domain and the relationship between them. It represents knowledge as a hierarchy of concepts within a domain. It uses shared vocabulary to signify the types of ontologies, their types, properties, and the linkages between them. This chapter discusses the following:

- The concept of Ontologies and its characteristics;
- Relation of Ontologies to Big Data trend;
- Advantages and Limitation of Ontologies; and
- Application of Ontologies.

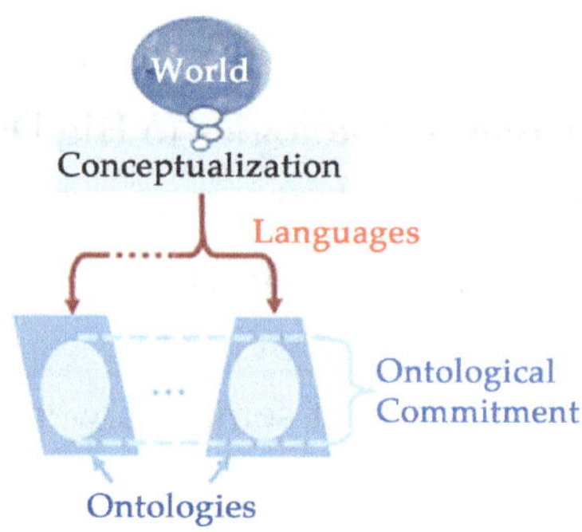

4.1. CONCEPT OF ONTOLOGIES

Ontologies represent structural frameworks which facilitate in organizing information. They are commonly used in artificial intelligence, systems engineering, sematic web, software engineering, enterprise bookmarking and library science as a form of knowledge representation about the world or a part of it.

The components such as individuals, classes, attributes, and relations have to be specified formally. The rules, axioms, and restrictions also have to be specified. Consequently, ontologies do not just introduce a shareable and reusable knowledge representation but add new information as well. Various methods exist which use the formal specification for knowledge representation. For example, taxonomies, vocabularies, topic maps, thesauri, and logical models are some methods. However, ontologies differ from taxonomies or relational database schemas because unlike them, ontologies express relationships. This facilitates users to link multiple concepts to other concepts in many ways.

Ontologies can be considered as one of the building blocks of Sematic Technologies. They are a part of the W3C standards stack for Sematic Web. They provide users with the required structure to link one piece of information to others on the Web if Linked Data. An important feature of ontologies is that it enables database interoperability, seamless knowledge management and cross-database search. This is possible because ontologies are used to specify common modelling representation of data from heterogeneous database systems.

Learning Activity
The Use of Ontologies
Enumerate the various ontologies that maybe involved in the data related to a firm that is given the responsibility of collecting data on the people eligible to vote in the elections of a nation.

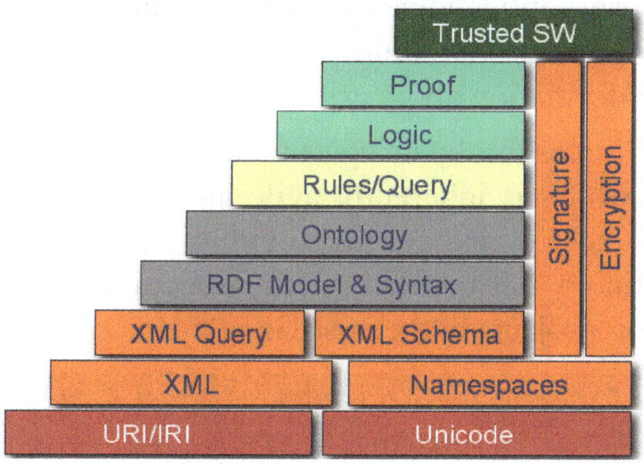

4.1.1. Characteristics of Ontologies

The important traits of ontologies are that they make explicit domain assumptions and facilitate a common understanding of knowledge. Consequently, the interoperability of the interconnectedness of the model makes it suitable for dealing with the difficulties experienced in accessing and querying data in large organizations. Ontologies also improve provenance and metadata. This allows the organizations to comprehend the data better and enhance data quality.

4.2. RELATION OF ONTOLOGIES TO BIG DATA TREND

Many experts believe that the role that ontologies plays in applications is comparable to the role of Google on the web. Ontology facilitates users to search for a schematic model of all data within the applications. They extract the required data from a source application. These applications could be big data applications, CRM systems, warranty documents, files, etc. These extracted semantics are linked to a search graph and not a schema. This provides the desired results to the users.

Ontology enables a user to adopt a different technique of using enterprise applications. It eliminates the need to integrate various applications. Users using ontology can search and link applications, files, spreadsheets, databases anywhere.

Ontology has displayed considerable potential in the past years. Many organizations have developed applications for different requirements that have been developed and used by organizations.

In order to obtain an organization-wide integrated view requires an integration of these applications which is a difficult task, expensive, and also risky. Ontology does not require integration of systems and applications when gathering information about critical data or trends.

Ontology facilitates this by using a unique combination of a graph-based semantic model which is inherently agile and semantic search. The time involved and the cost of integrating complex data is greatly reduced. In other words, Ontology has revolutionized data correlation, data acquisition and data migration projects in the post-Google era.

4.3. ADVANTAGES AND LIMITATIONS OF ONTOLOGIES

The ontologies have several advantages and limitations which are discussed below.

4.3.1. The Benefits of Using Ontologies

- A key trait of ontologies is that it establishes essential relationships between concepts built into them. This helps in the automated reasoning of data. This reasoning can be easily implemented in a sematic graph database that uses ontologies as their semantic schemata.
- Experts point out that ontologies' functions are similar to the human brain. The way they work and reason with concepts is comparable to the way humans comprehend interlinked concepts.
- Ontologies can not only be used for reasoning, but they also provide intelligible and simple navigation for users to move from one concept to another in the ontology structure.
- Another benefit of using ontologies is that they are easy to extend. This is because relationship and concept matching can be added to the existing ontologies easily. This model evolves as data grows with minimum impact on dependent processes and systems even if there is an error or something needs to be changed.
- Ontologies facilitate the representation of any data format, whether it is structured, unstructured or semi-structured. This enables seamless data integration, easier concept and text-mining and data-driven analytics.

4.3.2. Limitations of Ontologies

Undoubtedly, ontologies provide various tools for modeling data. However, they have their own limitations.

- One limitation of ontology is the lack of property constructs.

Example of Class Construct

OWL2, which is an updated version of Web Ontology Language, offers a powerful class construct, however, it has a limited set of property constructs. OWL is a semantic web computational logic-based language which provides consistent, detailed, and meaningful distinctions between classes, relationships, and properties.

- The second limitation arises because of the way the OWL employs constraints. They specify how data should be structured and does not allow data which is inconsistent with these constraints. This is not always am advantage. It is seen that the structure of the data imported from a new source into the RDF triple store is inconsistent with the constraints set using OWL. Therefore, it is required to modify this new data before integrating it into what is present in the triple store.

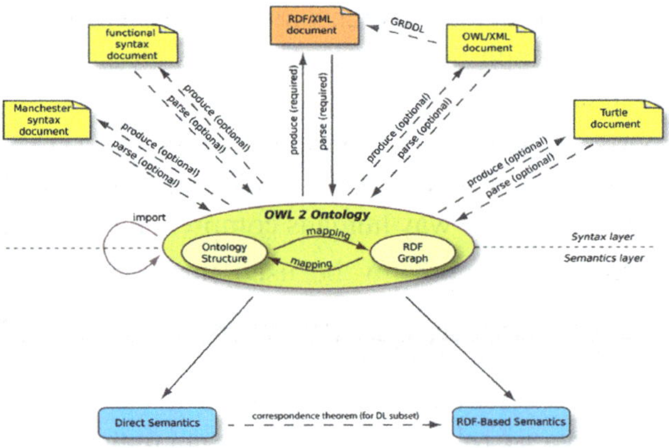

4.4. WHY ARE ONTOLOGIES DEVELOPED?

Ontologies define the terms which are used to describe and represent an area of knowledge. They are helpful in various applications to capture the relationship and improve knowledge management.

Ontologies are used in causality mining in pharma. The identified explicit relationships are categorized into a causality relation ontology. Ontologies are also used for semantic web mining, fraud detection, mining health records for insights, semantic publishing and fraud detection.

In simple words, ontologies provide a framework that represents reusable and shareable knowledge across a domain. They have the ability to describe relationships and high-quality interconnectedness. This makes them suitable for modeling high-quality, coherent, and linked data.

In recent times the development of ontologies has shifted from the realm of Artificial-Intelligence laboratories to desktop of domain experts. Ontologies are common in the World-Wide Web. The ontologies on the Web include large taxonomies categorizing Websites to the categorization of products on e-commerce sites.

The W3C is developing the Resource Description Framework (RDF). This is a language used for encoding knowledge on Web pages which makes it understandable to the users. The Defense Advanced Research Projects Agency (DARPA), is developing DARPA Agent Markup Language (DAML).

Many disciplines develop standardized ontologies. The domain experts use them to share and annotate information in their area of work. For example, the Medical field has developed standardized, structured vocabularies and semantic networks of the Unified Medical Language System.

Various general purpose ontologies are also being developed.

An ontology presents a common vocabulary for researchers who have to share information in a domain. Some of the objectives of developing an ontology are discussed below:

4.4.1. Sharing Common Understanding of the Structure of Information among People or Software Agents

This is a common goal in developing ontologies. For example, there are many websites providing medical information or medical e-commerce services. If all the sites share and publish the same underlying ontology of terms that they use, it will help the computer agents to extract and aggregate information from various sites. The agents can make use of this information as input data for other applications or respond to queries.

4.4.2. Enabling Reuse of Domain Knowledge

This is one of the major factors that drove the recent development in ontology research. For example, if a large ontology has to be developed, several existing ontologies can be integrated which describe parts of the large domain. General ontology like the UNSPSC ontology can be reused and used to describe other domains of interest.

4.4.3. Making Explicit Domain Assumptions

This is important for an underlying implementation as it facilitates the alteration of these assumptions if the knowledge about the domain also changes. If coding assumptions are rigid in a programming language, these assumptions not only become hard to find and comprehend, but also difficult to change. This is especially true for individuals who do not have programing expertise. Besides, explicit specification of domain knowledge also helps new users understand the meaning of the terms in the domain.

4.4.4. Separating the Domain Knowledge from the Operational Knowledge

Another reason why ontologies are commonly used is for separating domain knowledge from operational knowledge. A task can be described to configure a product from its components as per the specification and implement a program that configures the product and the components independently. An ontology of PC-components and their traits and apply the algorithm to configure a customized PC.

4.4.5. Analyzing Domain Knowledge

This is possible if the declarative specification of the terms is known. A formal analysis of these terms is extremely valuable when the existing ontologies are being reused or extended.

It is observed that the ontology of the domain is in itself rarely the goal. Developing an ontology is comparable with defining a set of data and their structures which enables other applications to use them. Domain-independent applications, and problem-solving methods, software agents use ontologies and the knowledge bases that are developed as data.

4.5. SEMANTIC WEB

Semantic web refers to the information that can be understood by human beings and cannot be understood by the machine because the data is without structure. Semantic web was initially developed to facilitate users with essential data on the internet and this data can be used to analyse and apply to different forms of data.

Learning Activity
Web Semantics
Track the importance of web semantics when applied to a Big Data. Locate the sector in which it is applicable and explain the reason for which it is applied in that sector.

RDF is the language that is used for the definition of data structure. The semantic web is known to be an extension of the present web technologies. The semantic web is known to provide the information in a well-defined manner and would facilitate human beings and computers to work in collaboration with one another. The novel web technologies that would come up will combine with the existing technologies along with knowledge representation formalisms. The semantic web is the web technology that has arrived by making gradual changes to the existing technologies.

Example of Semantic Web
Vodafone Live!, a multimedia portal for accessing ringtones, games, and mobile applications, is built on Semantic Web formats that enable subscribers to download content to their phones much faster than before. Harper's Magazine has harnessed semantic ontologies on its Website to present annotated timelines of current events that are automatically linked to articles about concepts related to those events.

It is generally seen that most of the people do not even know what actually the Semantic Web is. One of the best available definition was presented in the May 2001 in the Scientific American article "The Semantic Web" (Berners-Lee et al.) that says "The Semantic Web is an extension of the current web in which information is given well-defined meaning, better enabling computers and people to work in cooperation." People who have some experience in the Semantic Web have an in-depth understanding of what this broad statement means, and base their work on the famous "semantic web tower," a creation of Tim Berners-Lee's inspiring drawing on whiteboards. Even if anyone is not a geek, he or she might encounter the article on the semantic web, or followed some presentation, and then the person will definitely meet the tower, which is portrayed like this.

The presentation or article might have then explained a person about what the "layers" of this tower are, starting from the basic bricks (URIs and Unicode), up to XML, and then up to more and more sophisticated layers such as Ontology, RDF, and so on.

Now, after briefing with this, a person definitely knows how things work, and have been interested in converting this plan into real action. Or, in case a person does not know about this, then it might have been waiting for someone to show in a better way what it actually means. In fact, the plan that has been described above has been rapidly taking place: most of the slots are rapidly filling up (RDF Schema, RDF, Digital Signature and Ontology). Currently, there are many people who are eagerly waiting for this, and the Semantic Web has not yet taken off. What's the matter here?

4.5.1. "P" Axis

The concept has been taken out from the definition of Semantic Web that was described earlier: "The Semantic Web is an extension of the current web in which information is given well-defined meaning, better enabling computers and people to work in cooperation." Now, one of the primary known fact that the tower is filling up with the traditional established standards in accordance with the first part of the definition, "an extension of the current web." The fact that these standards are primarily dependent on the second part of the definition: "enabling computers to work in cooperation." The aspect that is missing in this is one of the most important parts of the definition: the people. Those people who are awaiting.

So, it is of not so much importance for those people that the slots work with computers: they want to be indulged or include in the game, they want the Semantic Web to fulfil its promise, to enable "computers and people to work in cooperation."

4.6. MAJOR COMPONENTS OF SEMANTIC WEB

The major components of the semantic web are as follows:

- XML: XML can be expanded as Extensible Mark-up language and it is a mark-up language like HTML, but the purpose of XML was different from HTML. XML was designed to transport and store data but it would not display data. This language has an elemental syntax for the content structure within documents.

- XML Schema: XML schema refers to a language that would provide a format for the structure and content of the components that are a part of the XML documents.
- RDF: RDF is expanded as RDF and it is known to be a language that is used to express several data models. RDF is known to be designed to provide information
- RDF Schema: RDF schema refers to the vocabulary that is used for describing different properties and classes for different resources that are dependent on RDF.
- OWL: OWL refers to a language which is called as the web ontology language. OWL refers to a general method by which a process is maintained for web information. The language OWL is known to have more vocabulary and strong syntax than RDF.
- SPARQL: SPARQL is known to be the protocol and query language that is used for several semantic web data sources.

The data that is being generated in every business transaction is huge and this data is not stored just in one computer, but it is accessed through the web from many computers and stored in these computers. The arrival of the latest technologies such as the internet, social media, and other web technologies makes it easy for people to store, upload, and access data. Web technologies have made it extremely easy and fast to access data. There are several researchers who have come up with the latest technologies to manage and organize data which is called as semantic web.

The semantic web has applications in several fields such as information systems, search engine and many other fields in the fields of data mining. One of the huge applications of the semantic web is in data mining because it facilitates the analysis of large volumes of data. The different syntaxes or formats of data in the semantic web will have specifications such as RDF/XML, N3, Turtle, N-Triples, and OWL. This is used for data analysis to identify the patterns or relationships in data, which is the biggest advantage of data mining.

The research in the field of semantic web is in a preliminary stage and the management tool for semantic is poor because of which the data that is stored in the semantic web is in a specific format that can be directly used in data mining. The research in the field of data mining suggests that several algorithms of the semantic web data are being used in data mining in some areas such as data classification, association rule mining and others.

4.7. CHECKPOINTS

1. Explain the term 'Ontology.'
2. Explain the basic concept of Ontologies.
3. Enlist the various characteristics of Ontologies.
4. What is the connection between Ontologies and Big Data trend?
5. What are the advantages of Ontology?
6. What are the limitations of Ontology?
7. Explain the term 'Semantic Web.'
8. Enlist the major components of Semantic Web.
9. What is the reason for the development of Ontologies?
10. What is the "P" axis in semantic web?

CHAPTER 5

Data Integration and Interoperability

LEARNING OBJECTIVE

In this chapter, you will learn about:

- The meaning of data integration;
- The various fields in which data integration takes place;
- The various kinds of data integration;
- Challenges in the integration of Big Data and interoperability;
- The model for logistic regression;
- Strategies and methods involved in reduction of data; and
- The meaning of datavisualization.

Keywords

Data Integration, Data Warehousing, Data Migration, Data consolidation, Data Propagation, Data Virtualization, Data Federation, Interoperability, Data Inconsistency, Immortality, Immutability, Data Objects, Data Record Reconciliation, Big Data Immutability

5.1. WHAT IS DATA INTEGRATION?

Data integration consists of merging the data from various sources, which are being stored with the help of several numbers of technologies and offers an integrated interpretation or understanding of the data. Data integration becomes more and more significant in cases of combining the systems of two companies or combining the applications within one company to provide a combined understanding or interpretation of the data assets of any company. The later initiative is sometimes known as the data warehouse.

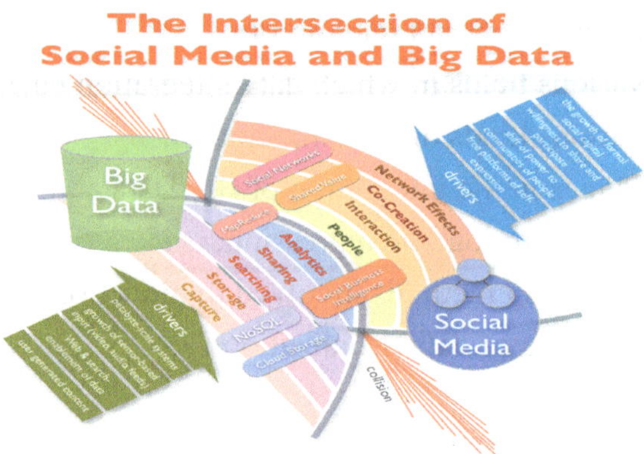

Probably the most well-known execution of the data integration is constructing a data warehouse of an enterprise. The advantage of a data warehouse is that, it permits a business to implement the analysis which is based on the data, available in the data warehouse. This implementation would not be possible to do on the data which is available only in the source system. The reason behind that is, the source systems probably may not comprise the corresponding data; nevertheless, the data saved with a similar name, can be referring to different entities.

Example of Data Integration in Rating Companies
Rating companies like Nielsen and Comscores take their reputation on having the-mostaccurate insights available. Collecting more data from more sources ensures that ratings are as comprehensive and trustworthy as possible. Deeper data also creates opportunities to rate new things in new ways. Constantly collecting more information is what will keep existing rating systems relevant.

5.2. DATA INTEGRATION AREAS

Data integration is a term which comprises the various numbers of different sub-areas which are mentioned below:

- Data warehousing;
- Data migration;
- Enterprise application/information integration; and
- Master data management.

5.2.1. Data Warehousing

A data warehousing is defined as a methodology for gathering and regulating the data from several numbers of different sources to offer purposeful business perceptions and understandings. A data warehouse is a combination of technologies along with several elements that support the strategic implementation of data.

The data warehouse is an electronic storage of a huge quantity of information by a business which is map out for query and analysis as an alternative to the process of a transaction. It is a course of transforming data into information and making it available to the users at the appropriate time to make a difference.

The decision support database (which is Data Warehouse) is sustained separately from the operational database of the organization. Nevertheless, the data warehouse is not a product but an environment. A data warehouse is an engineered structure of an information system that offers the users with the present as well as historical decision support information. This support information is quite difficult to access or present in the conventional operational data store.

The data warehouse is the core of the Business Intelligence (BI) system which is constructed for data analysis and reporting.

Data warehouse system is also known by the following name:

- Decision Support System (DSS);
- Management Information System;
- Analytic Application;
- Executive Information System;
- Business Intelligence Solution; and
- Data Warehouse.

5.2.2. Data Migration

Data migration is the process of moving the data between data storage systems, data formats or a computer system. The completion of the project of data migration is done for several numbers of reasons, which is consisting of swapping or upgrading the servers or the storage equipment, transferring the data to third-party cloud providers, website consolidation, infrastructure maintenance, application or database migration, software upgrades, company mergers or data centre relocation.

5.2.2.1. Types of Data Migration

Up-gradation of the System and cloud migrations offer the businesses with opportunities to show their quickness, improve growth, and the determine business significances. Data migrations help in reducing the quantity of capital expenses through the course of moving the applications to an enhanced and advanced environment.

There are three main types of data migration which are mentioned in the following table.

Cloud Migration	Cloud migration is the process of transferring the data, applications as well as all important business components from the on-premise data center to the cloud, or from one cloud to the other cloud.
Application Migration	Application migration is comprising the transfer of application programs to a modern environment. Application migration can transfer the complete application system from an on-premise IT center to the cloud or in between the clouds.
Storage Migration	Storage Migration is the process of transferring the data to a modern system from the arrays which are out of date or fashion. Storage migration also helps in the improvement of the performance during the course of offering scaling which is cost efficient.

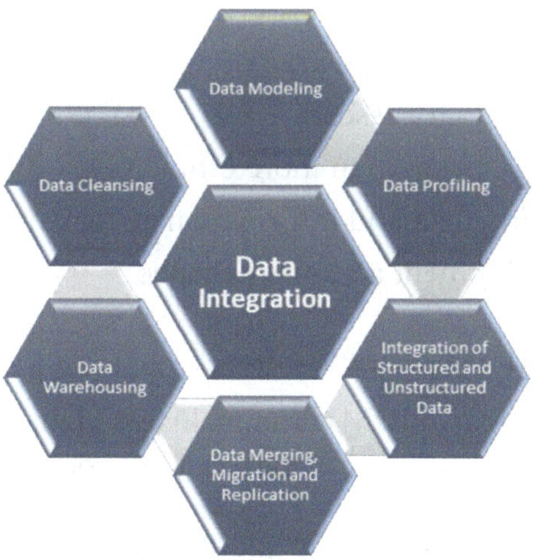

Several numbers of service providers offer business process migration which is associated with the business activities of an enterprise. Storage migration replaces and advances the tools which are used in business management and it helps in transferring the data from one database to the other database or from one application to the other application.

5.2.3. Enterprise Application/Information Integration

Enterprise application integration (EAI) is the implementation of the technologies and services across an enterprise that permits the combination of software applications as well as hardware systems. Several numbers of proprietary and open projects provide EAI solution support.

EAI is associated with the middleware technologies. Apart from the existing technologies based on EAI, other developing EAI technologies comprise the Web service integration, service-oriented architecture, content integration as well as business processes.

EAI encounters these challenges by fulfilling three main purposes, which are mentioned as below:

- Data Integration: Ensures consistent information across different systems;
- Vendor Independence: Business policies or rules regarding specific business applications do not have to be re-implemented when replaced with different brand applications; and
- Common Facade: Users are not required to learn new or different applications because a consistent software application access interface is provided.

The advantages of EAI are clear:

- Real-time information access;
- Streamlining processes;
- Accessing information more efficiently;
- Transferring data and information across multiple platforms; and
- Easy development and maintenance.

5.2.4. Master Data Management

Master data management (MDM) is an inclusive methodology of permitting a business to connect all of its important data to a common point of reference. When it is properly done, MDM enhances the quality of the data, through the course of the reorganization of the data sharing, across personnel and departments. Moreover, MDM can make it much easier with respect to computing in several system architectures, platforms as well as applications.

The advantages of MDM elevate as the number and multiplicity of the organizational departments, worker roles along with computing applications expand. For this reason, MDM is more likely to be of value to large or complex businesses as compared to small, medium-sized or simple businesses.

When companies integrate, the application or execution of the MDM offers challenges, as several units having the consideration of the meaning of terms and entities which are intrinsic to their businesses. But, in mergers, MDM offers benefits, as it can help minimize confusion and optimize the efficiency of the new, larger organization.

For maser data management to function at its best, personnel, and departments must be taught how the data is to be defined, formatted, stored, and accessed. Recurrent, coordinated updates to the master data record are also very important.

5.2.4.1. Architecture and Benefits of MDM

Learning Activity

Data Integration

Suppose, you are given the data of some people from different sources, that target a group of customers of a beverage brand focusing on some of their particular aspects and features. Find out, what tools you can use to integrate your data that has close to 60,000 inputs in it.

MDM is supposed to carry an approach that is systematic in nature with respect to the data integration that makes sure that, consistent use and reuse of data. Customer data, more specifically, is a concern, and this concern is intensified by the recent introduction of unstructured web activity data to a huge record of data types that are found in customer profiles.

5.3. TYPES OF DATA INTEGRATION

Data Consolidation	Data consolidation helps in physically brings the data together from various separate systems. Data consolidation helps in creating a version of the integrated data in one data store. Sometimes the main objective of data consolidation is to decrease the number of data storage locations. Extract, transform, and load (ETL) technology aids the integration of the data. ETL extracts the data from various numbers of sources, alters that data into an understandable format, and then moves that data to the other database or in the data warehouse. The ETL process cleans, filters, as well as transforms data, and then applies business rules before data populates the new source

Data Propagation	Data propagation is the implementation of applications to copy data from one location to the other location. Data propagation is event-driven and can take place synchronously or asynchronously. Most of the synchronous data propagation supports two-way data exchange between the source and the target. Enterprise application integration (EAI) and enterprise data replication (EDR) technologies aids in the process of data propagation. Enterprise Application Integration combines the application systems for the exchange of messages and transactions. It is sometimes used for real-time business transaction processing. The integration platform as a service (iPaaS) is a modern approach to EAI integration.
Data Virtualization	Virtualization uses an interface to offer a near real-time, combined or integrated understanding of data that is gathered or collected from several numbers of sources with various data models. Data can be accessed from one location but is not stored in that single location. Data virtualization retrieves and interprets data but does not need an even formatting or a single point of access.
Data Federation	Federation is technically a form of data virtualization. Data federation uses a virtual database and creates a common data model for the heterogeneous data with the help of several numbers of systems. Data is brought together and can be view or accessed from a single point of access. Enterprise information integration (EII) is a technology that aids the process of data federation.

5.4. CHALLENGES OF DATA INTEGRATION AND INTEROPERABILITY IN BIG DATA

Interoperability is one of the abilities to communicate, implement programs, or transfer the data, between several different functional units in a manner that needs the user to have little or no knowledge of the unique features of those units.

In the context of information systems, interoperability is the ability of diverse kinds of computers, networks, operating systems, and applications to work together in an effective manner, in the absence of prior communication, in order to exchange information in a beneficial and meaningful manner (Inproteo, 2005).

In the spatial context, spatial interoperability is defined as the ability of a spatial system or components of a spatial system, to provide spatial information portability and inter-applications cooperative process control" (Bishr, 1998). In addition to it, it is defined by ANZLIC (2005), as the ability to connect together spatial data, information, and processing tools among the different applications, irrespective of the underlying software and hardware system and their geographic location. According to ISO/TC 211, the spatial interoperability is:

- The capability to find out the information and processing tools, when they are required, irrespective of the location where they are physically located.

- The ability to understand and employ the explored information and tools, irrespective of the platform that supports them, whether it is local or remote.

- The ability to take part in a healthy marketplace, where goods and services are responsive to the requirements of consumers.

The main objective of Interoperability is to overcome the inconsistency among the different systems. In addition to this, there are different drivers and needs for interoperability which comprise of:

- Decrease costly data acquisition, maintenance, and processing.
- Provide direct, on-demand access that decreases the time and cost. On-demand spatial information means being able to access the wanted spatial information in its most current state, with correct representation when it is needed.
- Inspire vendor-neutral flexibility and extensibility of products. Vendor-neutral products comply with open standards and are independent from underlying software/hardware.
- Save time, money, and resources.
- Improved decision-making.

5.5. CHALLENGES OF BIG DATA INTEGRATION AND INTEROPERABILITY

There are many challenges in big data integration and interoperability. Some of the important challenges are as follows:

5.5.1. Accommodate the Scope of Data

The need to scale to accommodate the sheer scope of data and the formation of new domains inside the organization could be considered as another challenge for interoperability. One of the ways of addressing this challenge is by implementing the high performance computing environment and enhanced data storage systems such as hybrid storage device which has the characteristics of hard disk drives (HDD) and solid state drives (SSD), featuring decreased latency, high dependability and quick access to the data.

This could collect large data sets from several sources. Finding the common operational methodologies among the two domains for integration as well as implementing the query operations and algorithms could help meet the challenges that are posed by the large data entities.

5.5.2. Data Inconsistency

The data from several heterogeneous sources could give rise to inconsistency in data levels. Thus, it needs more resources in order to optimize the unstructured data. Structured data allows performing the query operations to analyze, filter, and make use of this data for purposes such as business decisions and organization abilities.

In this case, where the large data sets are included, unstructured data exist in the higher volumes. This can be located by the use of the tag and sort methods, permitting to search the data using keywords. In addition to it, the Hadoop methodologies such as Map Reduce, Yarn which attune the large data sets into subdivisions. This helps in easing the data conversions and schedule processes individually. Flume can be executed for the streaming of large data sets.

5.5.3. Query Optimization

Query optimization at each level of data integration and mapping components to the existing or a new schema that could influence the existing, and new attributes. One of the ways in which the challenge is addressed is decreasing the number of queries by the use of strings, joins, aggregation, grouping all the relational data. Parallel processing, where the asynchronous query operations are performed on individual threads, can have a positive impact on the latency and response time.

Implementing the distributed joins (hash, sort, merge) and determining the data which comprise of larger processing, consumes more storage resources, which is reliant on the kind of data. By the use of the higher-level query optimization techniques such as data grouping, join algorithm selection, join ordering can be executed in order to overcome this challenge.

5.5.4. Inadequate Resources

Inadequate resources for executing data integration, this mentions the absence of financial resources, absence of skilled specialists, implementation costs. Every association must examine its investment abilities in order to execute a new phase of the work environment to its present work system. The absence of financials is usually faced by the small segment organizations which are restricted to only certain domain; for instance: An organization that is restricted to the consulting.

In real-time these associations can organize the alterations in small intervals as this could fetch them additional time in order to attain back the invested resources. The absence of skilled professionals can not only delay the projects but also demoralize the ability of the organization to manage the projects. The skilled professionals in big data are difficult to find as data integration needs a high level of experienced or skilled professionals who in the past would have dealt with the integration module.

This can be curbed if the associations set up training modules for its staff. The implementation costs could be higher for the execution of data integration as this comprises of licensing new tools and technologies from the vendors. This cost could be shared when two diverse associations are included in the procedure of integration after the merger.

5.5.5. Scalability

Scalability issues crop up when the new data from several resources are combined with data from legacy systems. The organizational changes could have an impact on the efficiency of legacy systems as it passes through many updates and modifications to meet the needs of new technologies so as to be incorporated with it. The mainframe, one of the oldest technologies from IBM has been incorporated with big data tool Hadoop turning it to a high performance computing experience.

The ability of mainframe to collect large data sets and higher data streaming rates makes it adjustable to the new technology Hadoop. Hadoop provides a high-performance computing experience by allowing the operations on huge data sets. The multidimensional characteristic of Hadoop provides a better emphasis on data forms such as unstructured, semi-structured and structured data.

Hive can be executed as a query processing in Hadoop which typically comprises of the steps: query language to a web interface to JDBC ODBC to Metadata and finally the Hadoop cluster. Overall, this method provides a better vision for the association that is looking for large data storage systems incorporated with big data tools.

5.5.6. Implementing Support System

Organizations require to create a support system for managing the updates and error reporting in every single step of the process of data integration. This would require a training module for training the professionals in order to handle the error reporting. In addition to this, this may need a huge investment for an organization.

In order to address this challenge, organizations should execute the enhancements in their work system to adapt themselves to the increasing market trends. The execution of a Support system could assist in analysing the errors in the present architecture which could give them a scope for further updates or modifications. Although a high investment, this could still prove helpful for associations post the variations.

5.5.7. ETL Process in Big Data

Each data item goes through the process of Extract Load Transform (ETL), thus converting into a huge data set on a whole after the integration, this could have an impact on the data storage abilities of the database. The process of

Extract Load Transform (ETL) is suggested for data integration as it ETL guarantees a systematic and step by step method for data integration.

The extract performs the data recovery from the sources which is considered as its main feature. This operation does not have an impact on the data sources. The process of data extraction is performed when there is an update or incremental notification from the data systems. In the scenario, where it fails to determine the notification, the extraction is performed on the entire data.

Immutability is defined as the concept that data or objects should not be modified once they are created. This idea has been infused throughout computing, and it is considered as an essential tenant of functional programming languages. These languages such as Haskell, Erlang, and Clojure. Popular object-oriented programming languages, such as Java and Python, treat strings as immutable objects.

The concept of immutability has been put forth in order to make parallel programming easier and simple. The main challenge of parallelism is that coordinating actors read from a parallel program and convert it to a mutable state. Another example of immutability in practice is the version control system Git.

Learning Activity
Data Interoperability
Find two companies that make high use of data interoperability and mention the reasons as to why they do that. List the benefits it provides to them.

5.6. IMMUTABILITY AND IMMORTALITY

Each version in a Gilt repo is effectively a tree of pointers to immutable blobs and diffs. New versions introduce new blobs and diffs, but those necessary to produce the previous version remain intact and unchanged.

5.7. DATA TYPES AND DATA OBJECTS

Programs require the local program data to function properly. This local program data consists of byte sequences that are included in the working memory. Byte sequences that belong together are known as fields. These are characterized by a length, an identity (name), and – as an additional attribute

– by a data type. All programming languages have an idea that defines how the contents of a field are interpreted in accordance with the data type.

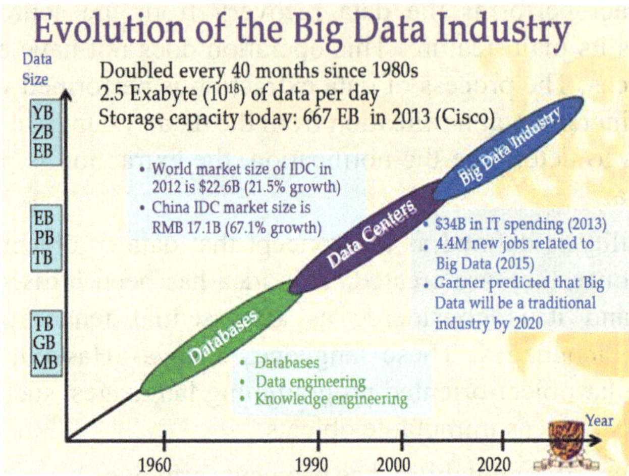

In the Advanced Business Application Programming (ABAP) type concept, fields are known as data objects. Therefore, each data object is considered as an instance of an abstract data type. There exist separate namespaces for data objects as well as data types which means that a name can be the name of a data object and the name of a data type at the same time.

5.7.1. Data Types

As well as occurring as attributes of a data object, data types can also be described independently. Then, the data types can be later on put to use in concurrence with a data object. The description or the meaning of a user-defined data type is totally based on the set of data types that are elementarily predefined.

One can describe the data types either locally in the declaration part of a program by the use of the TYPES statement) or it can also be described globally in the ABAP Dictionary.

On the other hand, one can use their own data types in order to declare data objects or to check the kinds of parameters that are present in generic operations.

5.7.2. Data Objects

Data objects are considered as the physical units with which ABAP statements (Advanced Business Application Programming) work at runtime. The memory space in the program is occupied by the contents of a data object.

These contents are accessed by ABAP statements. This is done by addressing the name of the data object and interpret them in accordance with the data type. For instance, statements can write the contents of data objects in lists or it can also be written in the database, this content can be passed to and received from routines. Also, the content can be changed by assigning new values to them, and they can relate them in logical expressions.

Each ABAP data object contains a set of technical attributes. These attributes are completely defined at the time when an ABAP program is running (field length, number of decimal places, and data type). One can declare data objects statically in the declaration part of an ABAP program (the most significant statement for this is DATA). It can also be declared dynamically at runtime (for instance, when once call procedures). As well as fields in the memory area of the program, the program also treats literals as data objects.

5.8. LEGACY DATA

A lot of data still exists on half-inch open reel tapes. Each standard that is widely used in the computer field hangs around for many years after it is no longer popular.

For a time, every single kid believes that the universe started with his own birth. Anything that has happened earlier to their birth is not real and of no consequence. Many Big Data resources have the same kind of disregard for events that preceded their birth.

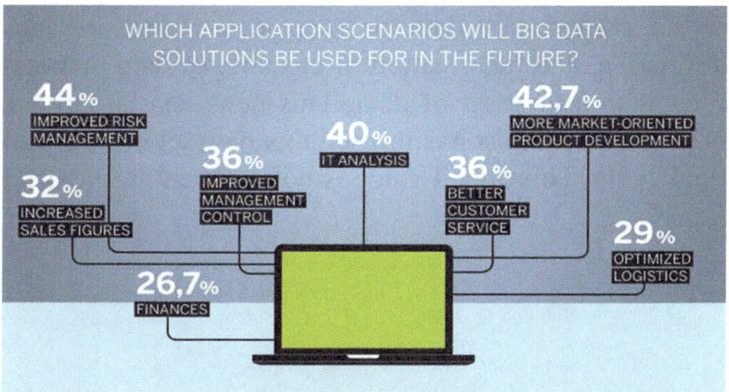

If events take place before the formation of the Big Data resource, they have no consequence and can be securely overlooked.

Here the main issue is that, for many domains, it is counterproductive to pretend that history begins with the formation of the Big Data resource. Take, for instance, patents. Anybody looking for a patent must determine whether his claims are, in fact, new, and this determination needs a search over the present patents.

For example, one day if the patent office of the U.S. decided to start computerizing all applications, it would require having some methods to add up all the patents dating back to 1790, when the initial patent act of the U.S. Congress was passed.

Some might claim that a good resource for U.S. patent data should comprise of patents granted within the original colonies; such patents date back to 1641.

Often, the Big Data creators disregard the legacy data. The old data that may be present in obsolete formats, on obsolete media, in the absence of proper annotation, and gathered under dubious circumstances. Old data frequently provide the only clues to time-dependent events.

In addition to it, Big Data resources typically absorb smaller resources or combine into larger resources with time. The managers of the resource must find a method to integrate legacy data into the aggregated resource if the added data is to have any practical value.

5.9. DATA BORN FROM DATA

The role of the data analyst is to extracts a large set of data from a Big Data resource. After subjecting the data to the numerous cycles of the usual operations (this comprise of data cleaning, data reduction, data filtering, data transformation, and the creation of customized data metrics), the data analyst is left with a new set of data. This new data is derived from the original set. The data analyst has infused this new set of data with some of the additional value. This added value is not apparent in the original set of data.

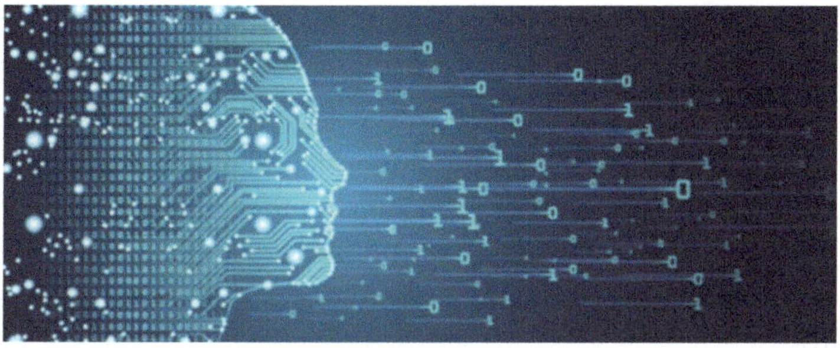

The main question is, "How does the data analyst insert the new set of derived data back into the original Big Data resource, without violating immutability?" The response is simplicity itself—reinserting the derived data is not possible and it should not be tried.

The transformed data set is not considered as a group of original measurements; it cannot be sensibly confirmed by the data manager of the Big Data Resource. The alterations assure that the data values will not fit into the data object model on which the resource was formed. There is no substitute for the original and primary data.

The role of the data analyst is to make their methods and the transformed data available for review by others. Every step that is included in making the new data set require to be recorded and explained in a careful manner, on the other hand, the transformed set of data cannot be absorbed into the data model for the resource.

The raw data were extracted for the original Big Data resource. The original Big Data resource can comprise a document that comprises the details of the analysis and the modified data set that is created by the analyst.

Alternately, the Big Data resource may provide a link to sources. These sources hold the modified data sets. These steps provide the general public with an information trail. This information trail leads from the original data to the transformed data. The transformed data is prepared by the data analyst.

5.10. RECONCILING IDENTIFIERS ACROSS INSTITUTIONS

In many of the scenarios, the biggest problem to attain the Big Data immutability is data record reconciliation. When the diverse institutions combine their data systems, it is critical that no data be lost, and all identifiers are preserved in a sensible manner.

Cross-institutional identifier reconciliation is defined as the procedure whereby institutions determine which of the data objects that are held in different resources, are similar in nature (that is the identical data object).

The data that is held in reconciled identical data objects can be merged in search results, and the similar data objects themselves can be combined (i.e., all of the encapsulated data can be merged in one data object) when Big Data resources are combined or when legacy data is absorbed into a Big data resource.

There exist no means to determine the unique identity of records (i.e., duplicate data objects may be present across institutions) in the absence of successful reconciliation. Also, the data users will not be able to analyse the data rationally that relates to or is reliant on the distinctions between the objects in a data set. For all practical purposes, there is no means to understand data received from numerous sources without data object reconciliation, Reconciliation is mainly significant for health care agencies. Some of the nations provide the inhabitants with a personal medical identifier. This medical identifier is used in every medical facility in the country. For instance, Hospital A can send a query to Hospital B for medical records relating to a patient who is present in the emergency room of Hospital A. The national patient identifier guarantees that the cross-institutional query will yield all of the data of Hospital B on the patient and will not comprise of the data on other patients.

Example of Google Making Use Of Big Data Techniques

Google's name is synonymous with data-driven decision making. The company's goal is to ensure all decisions are based on data and analytics. Infact, part of the company's culture is to discuss questions, not pithy answers, at meetings. Google created the People Analytics Department to help the company make HR decisions using data, including deciding if managers make a difference in their teams' performance. The department used performance reviews and employee surveys to answer this question. Initially, it appeared managers were perceived a sharing a positive impact. However, a closer look at the data revealed teams with better managers performed best are happier and work at Google longer.

5.11. SIMPLE BUT POWERFUL BUSINESS DATA TECHNIQUES

The data is what drives the world and also the data is analyzed every second. This is done whether by using the phone's Google Maps, the habits of Netflix or the online shopping cart and so many ways. Data is unavoidable and it's disrupting almost every known market.

The business world is now looking to the data with respect to market insights and eventually, in order to generate growth and revenue.

Despite the fact that the data is becoming the game change in the business world, it is important to note that the data is also being utilized by small businesses, corporate, and creative companies.

A global survey was done by McKinsey which shows that when the organizations use the data, it provides benefits to the customers and also the business and this is done by generating new data-driven services, by developing new models or strategies for the business.

There are five Big Data analysis techniques which are widely used:

- Association rule learning;
- Classification tree analysis;
- Machine learning;
- Regression analysis; and
- Descriptive Statistics.

5.12. ASSOCIATION RULE LEARNING (ARL)

Anomaly detection is an important part of data mining. This is defined as the procedure of searching for the items or events which do not correspond to a familiar pattern.

Such familiar patterns are referred to as anomalies and interpret critical as well as actionable data in a number of application fields. ARL searches for association into variables. There are a number of algorithms that are used in order to implement ARL.

5.12.1. Apriori Algorithm

A standard algorithm in data mining is the one named as apriori algorithm. This is used for the purpose of mining familiar items sets and appropriate association rules. It is developed in order to perform on a database that includes a number of transactions.

It is very important for Market Basket Analysis in an effective manner and it also helps in understanding which items customers will buy altogether.

It is also used in the field of healthcare in order to discover adverse drug reactions. Furthermore, it generates association rules which show all the combinations of medications and patients characteristics that help in drug-delivering in an effective manner.

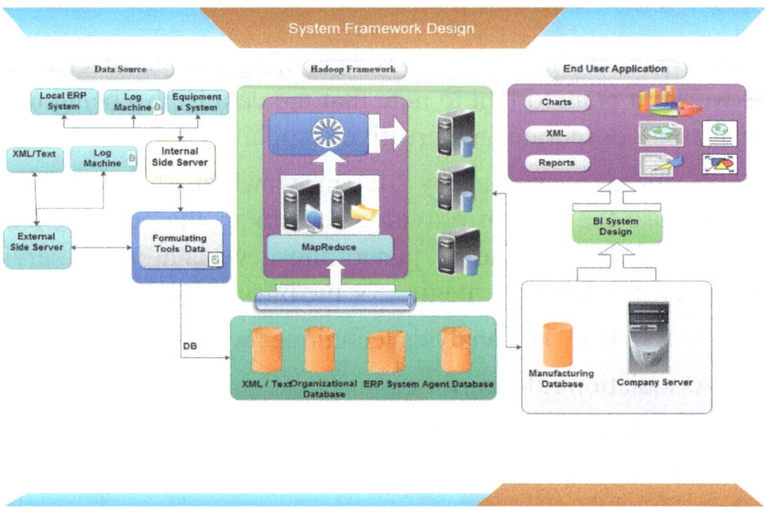

5.12.2. Eclat Algorithm

The application of the eclat algorithm is done in order to achieve the item set mining. Item set mining allows the user to obtain the periodic patterns in the data.

The main purpose of this algorithm is to use the set intersections in order to compute the support of a candidate item set and further avoiding the generation of subsets that does not exist in the prefix tree.

Eclat algorithm performs a depth-first search in order to count the columns. This is why the eclat algorithm performs faster than the Apriori algorithm.

5.12.3. F-P Growth Algorithm

The Frequent Pattern that is F-P Growth Classification is used with databases and not with the streams. The scans required by the Apriori algorithm is n+1 in case if a database is utilized, where n is the length of the longest model. By using the F-P Growth Method, the number of scans of the complete database can further be decreased to two.

5.13. CLASSIFICATION TREE ANALYSIS

A type of machine learning algorithm that is used in order to classify remotely sensed and ancillary data in support of land cover mapping and analysis is referred to as Classification Tree Analysis that is CTA.

The classification tree is the structural mapping of binary decisions that further lead to a decision about the class or interpretation of an object such as pixel.

Despite the fact that sometimes it is referred to as a decision tree, it is more a type of decision tree that can result in categorical decisions. Another form of the decision tree is a regression tree which results in quantitative decisions.

A classification tree consists of the branches which represent the attributes, while the leaves show the decisions. While using, the decision process starts at the trunk and further follows the branches until the time a leaf is reached.

Classification Tree Analysis that is CTA is an analytical procedure that takes examples of the known classes such as training data and further constructs a decision tree on the basis of measured attributes like the reflectance.

It is important the user should first use the training samples in order to grow a classification tree. This is known as the training step. After this, the whole image is classified by using this tree.

The second step of the Classification Tree Analysis is image classification. In this step, labeling is done to every pixel with a class while utilizing the decision rules of the previously trained classification tree.

First of all, the pixel is fed into the roots of a tree, the value in the pixel is checked in comparison to the value is already present in the tree and the pixel is sent to an internode which is done on the basis of where it falls in relation to the splitting point. The process work in continuation till the time when the pixel reaches a lead and then it is labeled with a class.

It is a kind of science which is not new but it is the one which gained fresh momentum. Since, a number of various machine learning algorithms have been around for a much long time, the ability to automatically implement the complex mathematical calculations to big data over and over and much faster which is a recent development.

5.13.1. Importance of Machine Learning Algorithms

The renewal in the interest in machine learning is because of the same factors which have made data mining and Bayesian analysis more popular than ever.

There are things such as growing volumes and varieties of available data, computational processing which is cheaper and more powerful and affordable data storage.

All of these things mean that it is possible to quickly and automatically produce the models which can analyze much bigger and more complex data and further fast delivery and can produce more accurate results even if it is done on a very large scale.

An organization has a better chance of identifying profitable opportunities or even avoiding unknown risks and this can be done by building precise models.

5.13.2. Machine Learning

A method of data analysis which automates the analytical model building is known as machine learning. It is the branch of artificial intelligence on the basis of the idea which systems can learn from the data, identify patterns and make decisions with minimal human intervention.

5.13.3. Evolution of Machine Learning

There is now a difference between machine learning today and machine learning which was in the past and the reason is the new computing technologies. It was born from the pattern recognition and the theory which the computers can learn without being programmed in order to perform particular tasks.

The iterative aspect of machine learning is important and the reason is they become able to independently adapt because the models are exposed to the new data. They tend to learn from the previous computations in order to produce reliable, repeatable decisions and results.

5.13.4. Regression Analysis

A form of machine learning in which the user tries to predict the continuous value based on some variables, this is known as regression. It is a kind of supervised learning in which a model is taught by using some features from existing data.

The regression model can build its knowledge base from existing data. On the basis of this knowledge base, the model can afterwards make predictions for the outcome of new data.

Continuous values are the numerical or quantitative values that are required to be predicted and are not from an existing set of labels or the categories.

There are a number of various examples of regression in which it is heavily used on a daily basis and in many cases, it has a direct business impact.

5.13.5. Descriptive Statistics

By using the frequency distribution, the user can easily figure out the frequency of the values observed. The measures such as the central tendency and dispersion can be used in order to learn more about the data for the given parameter.

There are three measures that can further be used for the central tendency that is mean, median, and mode.

Mean can be defined as the average value. It is equal to the sum of all the values divided by the number of observations. It is considered as the most popular measure of the central tendency, especially in the case when the data set does not have an outlier.

Median can be defined as the value in the middle when all the values are lined in order (assumption made is that there is an odd number of values). If in case there are even number of values then the median is the average of the two numbers in the middle.

It is very useful in the case when the data set has an outlier and the values are distributed very unevenly.

A mode is said to be the value that is observed most often. This tool is useful when the data is non-numeric or when asked to find the most popular item.

The basic measures of dispersion are the range and standard deviation. The larger the range and larger the standard deviation, the more dispersed the values are. The range can be defined as the difference of the maximum value and the minimum value for the variable.

5.14. CHECKPOINTS

1. Define the term Data Integration.
2. In respect to areas of Data Integration, explain the following term:
   i) Data warehousing;
   ii) Data migration;
   iii) Enterprise application/information integration; and
   iv) Master data management.
3. What are the different types of Data Integration?
4. Define the term 'Interoperability.'
5. What are the major challenges of Data Integration and Interoperability?
6. Explain the term Data Inconsistency.
7. Define the following term:
   i) Immortality; and
   ii) Immutability.
8. What are Data types and Data Objects?
9. Explain the term Legacy Data.
10. What is Data Record Reconciliation?
11. Why is Data Record Reconciliation a problem for Big Data Immutability?
12. What are the major Big Data analysis techniques that are used in Business World?

CHAPTER 6

Clustering, Classification, and Reduction

LEARNING OBJECTIVE

In this chapter, you will learn about:

- The predictive learning model through logistic regression;
- The meaning of data reduction;
- The various strategies involved in data reduction;
- The methods undertaken in data reduction; and
- The meaning of data visualization and the related aspects.

Keywords

Data Reduction, Data Visualization, Association rule learning, Classification tree analysis, Machine learning, Regression analysis, Descriptive Statistics, Logistic Regression, Decision Trees, Clustering Algorithms

INTRODUCTION

The main purpose of clustering and classification algorithms is to make sense of and further extract value from a large set of structured as well as unstructured data. If there are huge volumes of unstructured data, it can only make sense to try to part the data into some sort of logical groupings prior to attempting to analyze it.

Data mining techniques are majorly known as knowledge discovery tools for various purposes. Clustering is considered one of them. It is defined as a method in which the data are divided into groups in a way in which objects in each group share more similarity in comparison to other objects in other groups.

Data clustering is a well-known technique in various areas of computer science as well as related domains. While considering the classification, the idea is to predict the target class by analysis of the training dataset. This can be done by finding the proper boundaries for each target class.

Market Potential (Universe): People 16 years +
Segmentation: Demographic (multiple variables)
Variables: Occupation and income

Generally saying, the training data set is used in order to get better boundary conditions and this can be used so as to determine each target class. Once, the boundary conditions are determined, the next task is to predict the target class. This whole process is referred to as classification. Clustering and classification allow the user to take a glance at the data and then form some logical structures which are based on what you find there before going deeper into the nuts-and-bolts analysis. This is a classification technique that is based on Bayes's theorem along with an assumption of independence among the predictors. In other words, it can be said that the Naïve Bayes's Classifier assumes that the presence of any specific feature in a class is not related to the presence of any other feature.

Even though, these features depend on each other or upon the existence of the other features, the contribution is made by all of these properties independently to the probability.

It is quite easy to build and it specifically useful for a very large data set. In addition to the simplicity, Naive Bayes is also known for outperforming even the high sophisticated classification methods.

6.1. LOGISTIC REGRESSION (PREDICTIVE LEARNING MODEL)

This is a statistical method in order to analyze a data set in which there are one or more independent variables that can determine an outcome. The measurement of the outcome can be done with the help of the dichotomous variable.

The aim of the logistic regression is to find the best fitting model in order to describe the relationship between the dichotomous characteristics of interest and a set of independent variables.

This method is better in comparison to other binary classification such as nearest-neighbor because it also explains quantitatively the factors which result in the classification.

Example: Amazon product recommendations.

Ever wonder how Amazon displays products you make like on your return visit to their online store? It is because the store uses machine learning to track your previous interaction, learn your preferences and purchase behaviours from it. Based on these insights, the store customizes and personalizes your next visit with recommendations.

6.1.1. Nearest Neighbor

The k-nearest-neighbors algorithm is a classification algorithm, and also, it is supervised. It takes a number of labeled points and further, uses them in order to learn the way to label other points.

It looks at the labeled points which are closest to a new point in order to label that new point and then those neighbors vote. So, whichever label gets the most of the neighbor's vote, it is the label for the new point.

6.1.2. Support Vector Machines

"Support Vector Machine" (SVM) is defined as a supervised machine learning algorithm that can be used for both classifications as well as regression challenges. Furthermore, it is mostly used in classification problems.

In this algorithm, each data item is plotted as a point in n-dimensional space (where n is the number of features that the user has) with the value of each feature being the value of a specific coordinate. Then, the user performs classification and this is done by finding the hyper-plane which differentiates the two classes very well.

6.1.3. Decision Trees

The classification or regression models are built by the decision tree in the form of a tree structure. It breaks down a data set into much smaller subsets, simultaneously; the development of an associated decision tree takes place. The final result thus formed is a tree with decision node and leaf nodes.

The decision node consists of two or more branches and a leaf node is what represents a classification or decision.

The topmost decision node is a tree that corresponds to the best predictor which is known as the root node. The decision tree can handle both the categorical as well as numerical data.

6.1.4. Random Forest

Random forests are also known as random decision forests which are an ensemble learning method for the purpose of classification, regression, and some other tasks which operate by constructing a multitude of decision trees at the time of training and resulting the class which is the mode of classes that is classification or mean prediction that is regression of the individual trees.

6.1.5. Neural Networks

A neural network contains units which referred to as neurons which are arranged in layers, which further convert an input vector into some output. Each unit takes an input and then applies an (often nonlinear) function to it and then passes the output on to the next layer.

Generally, the networks are considered to be feed-forward. A unit feeds its output to all the units on the next layer. Despite this, there is no feedback to the previous layer.

Application of Classification Algorithms

- Bank customer's loan pay bank willingness prediction;
- Email spam classification;
- Cancer tumor cells identification;
- Facial key points detection;
- Drugs classification;
- Pedestrian detection in automotive car driving; and
- Sentiment analysis.

6.2. CLUSTERING ALGORITHMS

6.2.1. K-Means Clustering Algorithm

It can be said that the k-means clustering algorithm is probably the most well-known clustering algorithm. It is taught in a number of introductory data science and machine learning classes.

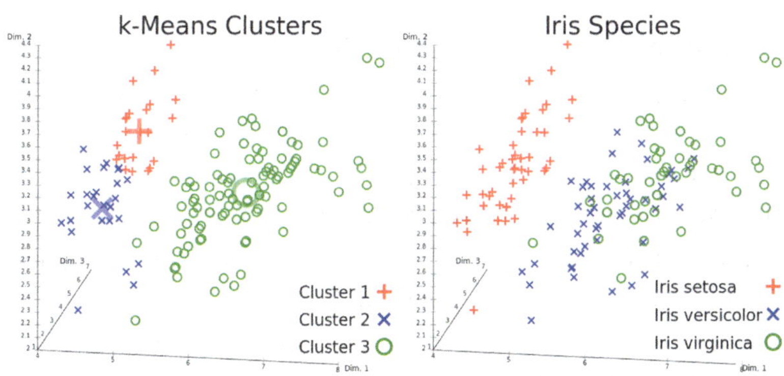

There is an advantage if k-means that if it is pretty fast because what we are really doing is computing and distances between the points and the group centers and so there are a few computations only. Thus, it does contain a linear complexity.

6.2.2. Mean-Shift Clustering

Mean shift clustering is based on the algorithm of sliding-window which attempts in order to find the dense areas of data points. It is basically a centroid based algorithm that means that the goal is to locate the center points of each group or class, which works by updating candidates for center points to be the mean of the points in the sliding-window.

The window of these candidates is then filtered in the post-processing stage in order to eliminate the near duplicates and further forming the final set of center points and their corresponding groups.

6.2.3. Hierarchical Clustering Algorithm

Hierarchical clustering algorithms are generally divided into two categories. One is top-down and the other one is bottom-up.

Bottom-up algorithms treat each data point as a single cluster at the outset and then successively merge pairs of clusters till the time when all the clusters have been merged into a single cluster which contains all the data points. Therefore, the bottom-up hierarchical clustering is known as hierarchical agglomerative clustering that is HAC. Representation of this hierarchy of clusters is done as a tree or dendrogram. The root of the tree is the unique cluster which gathers all the samples, the clusters are the leaves with only one sample.

6.2.4. Gaussian (EM) Clustering Algorithm

More flexibility is provided by the Gaussian Mixture Models (GMMs) in comparison to the k-means. From the GMMs, it is assumed that the data points are the Gaussian distributions. This is considered as a less restrictive assumption rather than saying that they are circular by using the mean.

So, there will be two parameters that should describe the shape of the clusters that is the mean and the standard deviation.

So, as to find the parameters of the Gaussian for each cluster, an optimization algorithm known as Expectation – Maximization that is EM will be used.

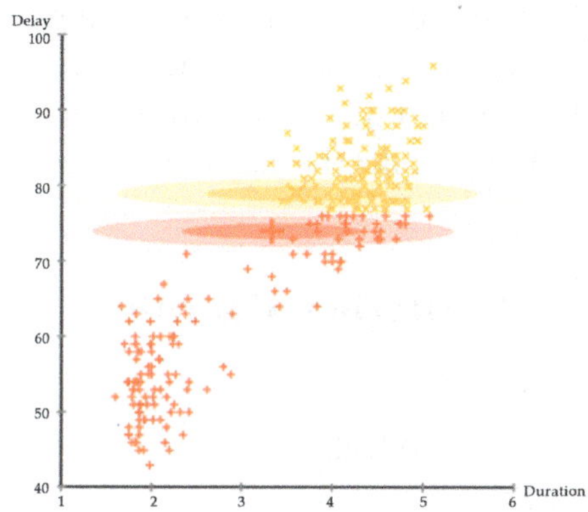

6.2.5. Quality Threshold Clustering Algorithm

By using the quality threshold, the QT-clustering is guided which in standard specification determines the maximum radius of the clusters.

The cluster radius is referred to as the maximal distance which exists among the central element and any member of the cluster. The central element thus has minimal summary distance in comparison to other cluster members.

6.2.6. Density-Based Clustering Algorithm

The density-based clustering algorithm is a density-based clustered algorithm that is similar to the mean-shift but it has a couple of more advantages in comparison to mean-shift. The density-based clustering algorithm provides some great advantages in comparison to some other clustering algorithms.

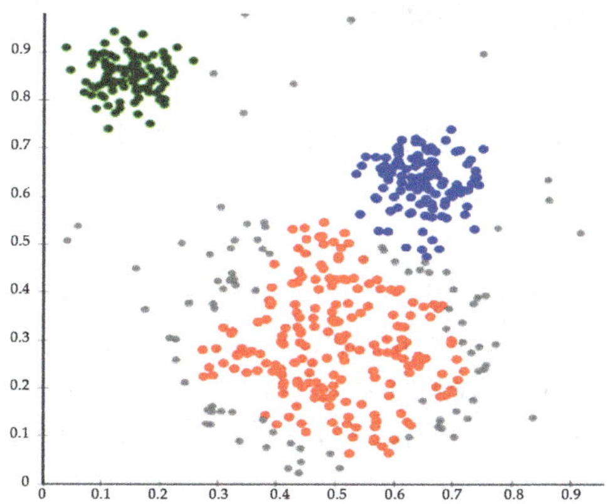

This clustering algorithm does not require a number of clusters per set. It also identifies outliers as noises, not like mean-shift which simply throws them into a cluster even though the data point is very different. In addition to this, it is able to find the arbitrarily sized and arbitrarily shaped clusters in a good manner.

6.2.7. Application of Clustering Algorithms

- Anomaly detection;
- Human genetic clustering;
- Recommender systems;
- Genome Sequence analysis;
- Grouping of shopping items;
- Analysis of antimicrobial activity;
- Search result grouping;
- Crime analysis;
- Climatology; and
- Slippy map optimization

Data reduction is considered as an umbrella term for a suite of technologies that comprise compression, de duplication, and thin provisioning. This serves to decrease the storage capacity that is needed to manage a given data set.

Therefore, storage vendors will define their storage offerings both in terms of raw capacity as well as post-data reduction, effective capacity. Data reduction is considered as the main factor in making all-flash solutions accessible for a variety of budgets.

6.3. DATA REDUCTION STRATEGIES

Pure Storage offers the most granular and complete data reduction of the industry by means of Flash Reduce, which is involved with every Flash Array purchase. For virtually any application, Flash Reduce provides the data reduction savings that bring the cost of all-flash under that of spinning disk. This is accessible even to small- and medium-sized enterprises. It has been observed that on average, Pure Storage provides a 5:1 ratio of data reduction.

Terabytes of data are stored in a database or data warehouse. Therefore, it may take very long to perform the process of data analysis and mining on such large amounts of data.

The techniques of data reduction can be applied in order to attain a compact representation of the data set that is much smaller in volume but still, it comprises critical information, yet it closely maintains the integrity of the original data. That is, the process of mining on the reduced data set should be more effective yet produce the same (or nearly the same).

Strategies for data reduction comprise of:

- Data cube aggregation — aggregation operations are implemented to the data in the creation of a data cube.
- Attribute subset selection — irrelevant, weakly relevant or redundant features or dimensions may be discovered and eradicated.
- Dimensionality reduction — encoding mechanisms are used in order to decrease the size of the dataset.
- Numerosity reduction — data is substituted or estimated by alternative, smaller data representations like the parametric models (which need to store only the model parameters instead of the actual data) or it is substituted or estimated by nonparametric methods like clustering, sampling, and the use of histograms.
- Discretization and concept hierarchy generation — raw data values for attributes are substituted by series or higher conceptual levels.

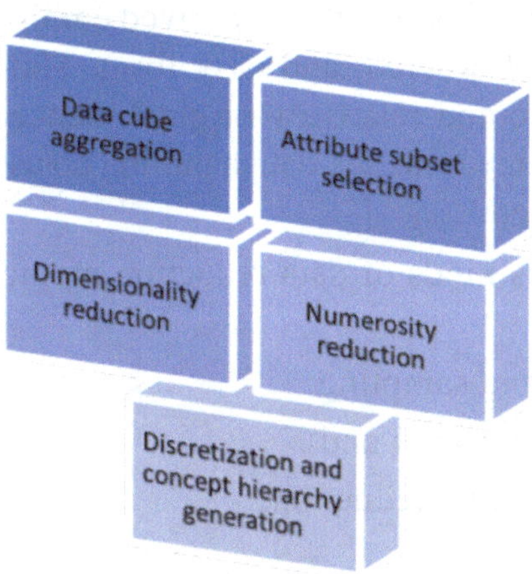

Data discretization is considered as a form of numerosity reduction that is very beneficial for the automatic generation of concept hierarchies. Discretization and concept hierarchy generation is considered as powerful tools for the process of data mining, in that they permit the mining of data at multiple levels of abstraction.

The computational time that is spent on the process of data reduction should not outweigh or remove the time that is saved by mining on a reduced data set size.

Learning Activity

Prediction of Data

Suppose you are the manager of a team that integrates data and provides solutions to the clients across various verticals. Your team has integrated the data from various sources on the products related to personal wellness. What are the possible verticals of the product on which you can give the predictions?

6.4. DATA REDUCTION METHODS

Many data scientists or experts make use of large data size in volume for the process of analysis, which takes a long time, though it is very hard to examine the data at some point in time. In data analytics applications, if the individual makes use of a huge amount of data, it may generate redundant outcomes. In order to overcome such type of problems, one can make use of the data reduction methods.

Data reduction is the process of transformation of numerical or alphabetical digital information that is derived empirically or experimentally into a corrected, well-ordered, and easy form. The decreased data size is very small in volume and relatively original, hence, the storage efficiency will rise and at the same time, the data handling costs along with the analysis time can be minimized.

There are various kinds of data reduction methods, which are listed as follows:

- Filtering and sampling;
- Binned algorithm; and
- Dimensionality reduction.

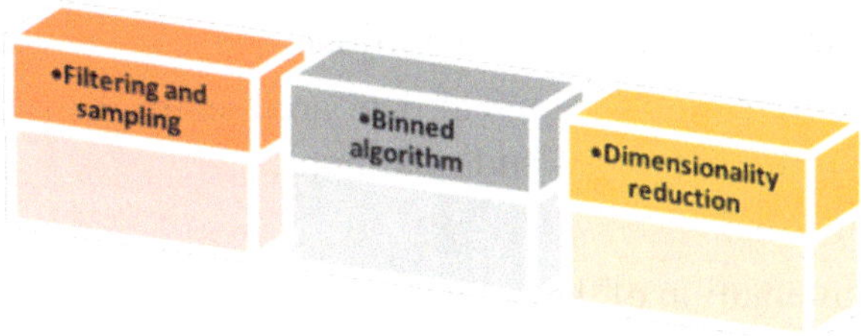

6.4.1. Five Reduction Technologies

There are data reduction strategies available for virtually any application: pattern removal, deduplication, compression, deep reduction, and copy reduction.

Always-On – Purity Operating Environment is designed in order to support high-performance, always-on data reduction. All of the performance benchmarks are taken with data reduction on.

Global – Unlike some data reduction solutions which function inside a volume or a pool, thus dividing the data and dramatically decreasing the dedupe savings, Purity Reduce dedupe is inline and global.

Variable Addressing – Purity Reduce scans for duplicates at the 512-byte granularity and auto-aligns with application data layouts in the absence of any tuning at any layer. In addition to this, variable (byte-granular) compression evades diluting the savings with waste that fixed-bucket granular compression implementations propagate.

Multiple Compression Algorithms – The diverse types of data compress in a different manner. Purity employs multiple compression algorithms for the purpose of optimal data reduction.

Designed for Mixed Workloads – Purity Reduce provides the optimum data reduction savings for mixed workloads without the need for any trade-offs and/or tuning.

6.5. DATA VISUALIZATION: DATA REDUCTION FOR EVERYONE

Data reduction, or the distillation of multitudinous data into meaningful parts, is playing an increasingly a significant part in recognizing the world and enhancing the quality of life. Consider the following examples:

- Categorizing space survey results to better describe the structure of the universe and its evolution;
- Examining the biological data and health records of the patients for better diagnosis and treatment;
- Programs;
- Segmentation of the consumers which is based on their behaviour and attitudes;
- Improved understanding of the nature of criminal activities in order to enhance the counter measures; and
- Optimizing mineral exploration efforts and decoding genealogy.

Learning Activity

Data Visualization

Find out at least three recent instances where data visualization has played a vital role in providing a stand to the business and predicting the future possibilities successfully.

Example of Data Visualization: U.S. Thanksgiving on Google Flights

Here's a great way to visualize things moving around in space over a given time. This one is powered by Google Trends, which tracked flights as they few to, from, and across the United States on the day before Thanksgiving. The visualization starts at the very beginning of the day and plays like a movie as time goes on, showing flights moving around the country. Without showing any numbers beside the time, viewers can see which times of day are more popular for international flights, for domestic flights, and for flights to and from different hubs around the country.

6.5.1. Proliferating Techniques

The huge number of use cases has led to a proliferation in data reduction techniques. Many of this come under the umbrellas of data classification and dimension reduction.

6.5.2. Exploring Differences

Deciding on the most suitable or appropriate data reduction technique for a specific situation can be daunting, making it tempting to simply depend on the familiar. Though, the diverse methods can generate significantly different outcomes.

In order to make the case, one needs to compare K-means and agglomerative hierarchical clustering (AHC) to part the countries based on export composition. The different configurations of principal component analysis (PCA) are also compared in order to determine underlying discriminators.

Data are drawn from the OECD Structural Analysis (STAN) Database. In addition to it, this Data is analyzed with XLSTAT, an easy-to-use Excel add-in.

6.5.3. Analytical Considerations

There exist no hard and fast rules regarding what data reduction method is best for a specific situation.

Though, there are some general considerations that should be kept in mind:

- Exploration and theory: Provide the degree to which outcomes can differ by technique, data reduction exercises are best treated as exploratory. Openness to trying the diverse methods is suggested rather than depending on the single method as the be-all and end-all. This does not negate the significance of having a theoretical foundation in order to shape discovery. Techniques or methods like cluster analysis and PCA will group any data and compress it. In the absence of a priori assumptions and hypotheses, analysis can turn into a wild goose chase.
- Sparsity and dimensionality: Data with restricted variation are likely to add little value to data reduction exercises. It can be considered for exclusion. At the other end of the spectrum, too much dimensionality can make the efforts complicated. Discerning which characteristics are most significant up-front and preparing data accordingly play a significant part in effective analysis.
- Scale, outliers, and borders: Consistent scales are needed so that the variables having a high amplitude or degree do not dominate. Also, Outliers can skew outcomes. For instance, because K-means divides the data space into Voronoi cells, extreme values can result in odd groupings.

At the same point of time, carte blanche removal of outliers is not suggested given the visions that potentially exist in exceptional cases. The other challenge with K-means is the potential to inaccurately cut borders among the clusters as it tends to make the partitions of a similar size.

6.6. CASE STUDY: COCA-COLA ENTERPRISES (CCE) CASE STUDY: THE THIRST FOR HR ANALYTICS GROWS

"It's a great opportunity for HR, and we should not pass upon it, because, if executed well, HR analytics combined with business data allows us to highlight the impact of people on business outcomes. It's about small steps, pilots, where you start to demonstrate the power of combining HR and business data.

If you understand the business problems and can come to the table with insights that had previously not been seen you enhance HR's credibility and demonstrate the value we can add as a function. What amazes me as an HR professional, with a lean six sigma background, is that companies are often great at measuring and controlling business processes but very rarely consider the importance of people in that process. People are without a doubt, one of the most important variables in the equation."

6.6.1. Data Analytics Journey

The HR analytics journey within Coca-Cola Enterprises (CCE) really began in 2010. Given the complexity of the CCE operation, its global footprint and various business units, a team was needed which was able to provide a centralized HR reporting and analytics service to the business.

This led to the formation of an HR analytics team serving 8 countries. As a new team, they had the opportunity to work closely with the HR function to understand their needs and build a team not only capable of delivering those requirements but also challenge the status quo.

"When I first joined CCE in 2010, it was very early on in their transformation program and reporting was transitioned from North America to Europe. At that point, we did not have a huge suite of reports and there was a limited structure in place. We had a number of scheduled reports to run each month, but not really an offering of scorecards or anything more advanced."

The first step was to establish strong foundations for the new data analytics program. It was imperative to get the basics right, enhance credibility, and automate as many of the basic descriptive reports as possible. The sheer number of requests the team received was preventing them from adding value and providing more sophisticated reports and scorecards.

CCE initiated a project to reduce the volume of scheduled reports sent to customers, which enabled them to decrease the hours per month taken to run the reports by 70%. This was a game-changer in CCE's journey.

Many of the remaining, basic, low value reports were then automated which allowed the team to move onwards in their journey and look more at the effectiveness of the HR function by developing key measures. The analytics team was soon able to focus on more "value-adding" analytics, instead of being overwhelmed with numerous transactional requests which consumed resources.

6.6.2. Standardizing and Reporting: Towards a Basic Scorecard

The team soon found that the more they provided reports, the more internal recognition they received. This ultimately created a thirst within HR for more data and metrics for measuring the performance of the organization from an HR perspective.

The HR analytics function knew this was an important next step but it wasn't where they wanted the journey to end. They looked for technology that would allow them to automate as many of these metrics as possible whilst having the capability to combine multiple HR systems and data sources.

A breakthrough, and the next key milestone in the journey for CCE, was when they invested in an "out of the box" system which provided them with standard metrics and measures, and enabled quick and simple descriptive analytics.

Instead of building a new set of standards from scratch, CCE piloted pre-existing measures within the application and applied these to their data. The result was that the capability to deliver more sophisticated descriptive analytics was realized quicker and began delivering results sooner than CCE business customers had expected.

"We were able to segment tasks based on the skill set of the team. This created a natural talent development pipeline and ensured the right skill set was dedicated to the appropriate task. This freed up time for some of the team to focus on workforce analytics.

We implemented a solution that combines data from various sources, whether it is our HR system, the case management system for the service centre, or our onboarding/recruitment tools. We brought all that data into one central area and developed a lot of ratios and measures.

That really took it to the next level." As with any major transformation, the evolution from transactional to more advanced reporting took time, resource, and commitment from the business, and there were many challenges for the team to overcome.

6.6.3. Consulting to the Business: HR as a Center of "People Expertise"

At CCE it's clear that HR analytics, insights, and combining HR and business data is an illustration of the value that HR can add to the business. CCE has developed a partnership approach which demonstrates the power that high quality analytics can deliver, and its value as a springboard to more effective HR practices in the organization.

By acting in a consultative capacity HR is able to better understand what makes CCE effective at delivering against its objectives, HR ensures both parties within the partnership use the data which is extracted, and find value in the insights which HR is developing. "To be a consultant in this area, you have to understand the business you're working in.

If you understand the business problem then you can help with your understanding of HR, together with your understanding of all the data sets you have available. You can really help by extracting the right questions. If you have the right question, then the analysis you are going to complete will be meaningful and insightful."

6.6.3.1. Moving from Descriptive Reporting Towards Correlation Analysis

There are numerous examples where the HR reporting and analytics team have partnered with the HR function and provided insights that have helped to develop more impactful HR processes and deliver greater outcomes for the business.

As with many organizations it is the engagement data with which the majority of HR insight is created. Developing further insight beyond standard survey outputs has meant that CCE has begun to increase the level of insights developed through the method, and by using longitudinal data they have started to track sentiment in the organization. Tracking sentiment alongside other measures provides leaders with a good indicator for sense checking the power of HR initiatives and general business processes. The question is whether the relationship between engagement and business results is causal or correlative. For CCE this point is important when explaining the implications HR data insights to the rest of the business.

6.6.3.2. Building Analytics Capability within HR at CCE

For CCE's analytics team one of the most important next steps is to share the experience and knowledge gained from developing the analytics function with their colleagues, and build capability across HR. "We are also reviewing the learning and development curriculum for HR to see what skills and competencies we need to build.

One of the competencies that we have introduced is HR professionals being data analysers. For me, it is not only understanding a spreadsheet or how to do a pivot table, but it is also more understanding what a ratio is, or understanding what their business problems are, or how data can really help them in their quest to find an intervention that is going to add value and shape business outcomes."

6.6.4. Utilizing Predictive Analytics: CCE's Approach

For organizations like CCE natural progression in analytics is towards mature data processes that utilize the predictive value of HR and business data. For most organizations this can too often remain an objective that exists in the far future, and one which without significant investment may never be realized. Alongside the resource challenges in building capability there also exists the need to understand exactly how data may provide value, and the importance of objective and critical assessment as to how data can be exploited.

Without an appreciation for methodological challenges, data complexity and nuances in analysis, it may be that organizations use data without fully understanding the exact story the data is telling. "Predictive analytics is difficult. We are very much in the early stages as we are only starting to explore what predictive analytics might enable us to do, and what insights it could enable us to have. If we can develop some success stories, it will grow. If we go down this route and start to look at some predictive analytics and actually, there is not the appetite in the business, or they do not believe it is the right thing to do, it might not take off. If you think about the 2020 workplace, the issues that we have around leadership development, multi-generational workforces, people not staying with companies for as long as they have done in the past, there are a lot of challenges out there for HR. These are all areas where the use of HR analytics can provide the business with valuable insights."

For CCE it appears that analytics and HR insight are gaining significant traction within the organization. Leaders are engaging at all levels and the HR function is increasingly sharing insights across business boundaries. This hasn't been without its challenges: CCE faces HR's perennial issues of technology and the perceived lack of analytics capability.

However, their approach of creating quality data sets and automated reporting processes has provided them with the foundations and opportunity to begin to develop real centers of expertise capable of providing high quality insight into the organization. It is clear CCE remains focused on continuing its HR analytical journey.

6.5. CHECKPOINTS

1. Explain the Classification Tree Analysis technique used in Business World.
2. Explain the terms:
   i.) Machine Learning;
   ii.) Regression Analysis; and
   iii.) Descriptive Statistics.
3. What is Data Clustering?
4. What is Predictive Learning Model?
5. Define Clustering Algorithms.
6. What are the applications of Clustering Algorithms?
7. Define the term Data Reduction.
8. What are the various Data Reduction Strategies?
9. What are the various methods used for Data Reduction?
10. Define the term Data Visualization.

CHAPTER 7

Key Considerations in Big Data Analysis

LEARNING OBJECTIVES

In this chapter you will learn about:

- The major considerations that are taken in Big Data Analysis;
- The Approach taken in the analysis of Big Data;
- The various dimensions in data complexities;
- The complexities related to Big Data; and
- The methods involved in the removal of complexities.

Keywords
Query Output Adequacy, Resource Evaluation, Over fitting, Internet of Things, Bigness Bias, Data Protection, Data Complexities, Budget, Visual Representation, Inaccessible data, One Data Platform, Disaster Recovery

INTRODUCTION

Big Data statistics are troubled by various intrinsic as well as intractable issues. When the amount of data is large, the analyst can find everything he finds lurking somewhere within. Such kind of findings may have statistical importance without having any kind of practical importance.

In addition to that, whenever a subset of a dataset is selected from a huge collection, there is no way of knowing the relevance of data which is excluded. Big Data is considered as a developing technology and its application holds a huge potential as well as benefits for the organizations. The power of this technology is something that is yet a major concern.

7.1. MAJOR CONSIDERATIONS FOR BIG DATA AND ANALYTICS

Big Data will stay forever. This means that the organizations need to be able to process and effectively utilize ever-increasing volumes of the information. In order to support this, there are some major considerations for Big Data strategies:

7.1.1. Use Big Data Structures That Support Your Aims

The notion of 'data needs' is very significant which is generally overlooked. There is nothing as an effective, one-size-fits-all Big Data solution. As an alternative, the data structure should directly support the sole business aims.

Never with a partner who has no will to apply a tailored approach to a particular situation. Same as no two businesses are the same, no two data solutions should be either. Always go for customized options and acquire a solution that incorporates directly with the identity of an organization.

7.1.2. Embrace IoT or Find Someone Who Can Embrace It for You

The Internet of Things or IoT signifies the future of Big Data as it is revolutionizing various industries present all around the world. By harnessing the IoT, several businesses are acquiring data directly from the source with no manipulation through third parties.

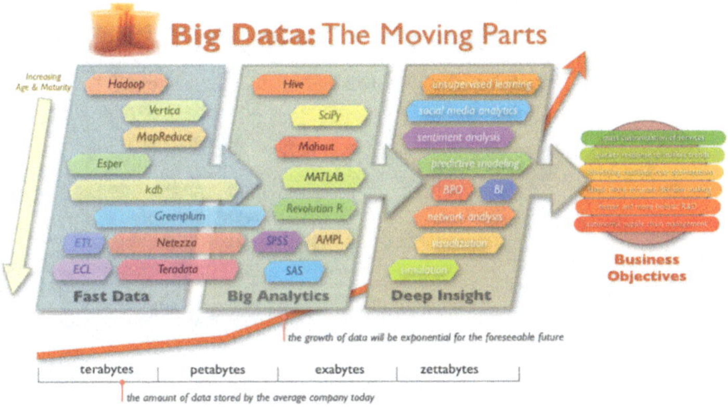

At present, there are an estimated 23.14 billion IoT-connected devices all around the world. This is a figure which is estimated to increase to 62.12 billion by the year 2024. All such devices are able to generate a huge number of data points.

When it is about IoT, management, and discernment of data are just as important as the collection of data. There is no shortage of data that is to be acquired from IoT. In addition, this volume is growing day by day. The outcome can be a vast pool of data that organizations are simply not prepared to deal with.

In this aspect, finding the right partner or the provider of data solution is very critical. IoT represents a huge vein of value that is waiting to be mined or extracted. It is also critical to determine which of the data sources comprise this value and which do not. Organizations are required to use IoT hardware wherever they can, or to be working with a partner who has the resources and scope they actually need.

7.1.3. Data Protection Is Paramount

The collection as well as the arrangement of data is very important in order to understand the requirements of customers. In addition to that, the protection of data is equally important. Fraud and theft related to corporate data have now become a major issue.

The consequences can be huge in the case of data theft. The particular organization will lose vital levels of status or respect in the market and the customers, partners, clients, etc. will be put at major risk.

Actually, the organization is mainly liable to be accused if it is found that it did not take the apt measures so as to assure data security and execute precautions on an institutional level.

Organizations must always assure that the protocols of data protection cover every single aspect of corporate architecture and should conduct assessments consistently so as to remove any kind of weak points.

7.1.4. Increase Your Network Capability

Big Data volumes are not decreasing. In its place, the data is coming at a rapid rate from an ever-expanding roster of sources. Considering this in mind, organizations are required to have data collection, its processing and storage protocols that can effectively deal with such kind of deluge.

Work with those partners that can basically provide different kinds of high-speed processing as well as high-level storage that the organizations need. It is not just that the Big Data volumes are growing, but the businesses too. It means that the scalability must always be at the forefront of the organizations' agenda.

Organizations should always make a long-term plan for Big Data strategy and the network architecture that can further support the predicted growth. They must be assured that the plan is able to provide an ongoing support to the organization along with its development.

7.1.5. Big Data Experience Cannot Be Underestimated

While selecting a data service provider or a partner, it goes with the more experienced option. The reason behind this is that Big Data is a very technical and rapidly developing field. In simpler terms, it is governed by the curves of development as well as trends that cannot be learned overnight.

Consider this into account while searching for a Big Data solutions provider and while employing specialists to work within the team. Observe their track record with an emphasis on genuine value creation from Big Data.

7.1.6. Be Flexible When It Comes to Storage

Storage demonstrates something of a conundrum for businesses looking to get the best results from the data. This is due to the fact that storage must be everything at once. It should always be ultra-secure; it should have the breadth and scope that is required to store ever-increasing volumes of the data; and it should always be easily accessible.

This is the main reason behind the requirement of a flexible approach for storage. The organizations are required to set up a physical, hybrid, and cloud storage structure together in a combination that suits the needs of data. Bringing this together can be very tough, mainly as the business grows in the market.

In addition to that, a harmonized approach is a major requirement. This kind of approach will see different components of the data storage strategy to work together. This can be acquired through the setup of the right kind of software. However, choosing a data solution provider who can effectively handle this for the organization is the most reliable as well as a cost-effective approach.

Learning Activity

Considerations in Big Data

Ponder over the ways in which taking the considerations mentioned above, into account, can help you in the business that you may be running. Consider that you are the owner of a food delivery app.

7.2. OVERFITTING

Over fitting basically takes place when a particular formula defines a set of data closely. It does not predict the behaviour of comparable data sets. In over fitting, the formula is used to define the noise of a specific system instead of the characteristic behaviour of the system.

Over fitting occurs with different kinds of models that principally do iterative approximations on training data, coming very closer to the training data set with each and every iteration. Neural networks are key example of a data modelling strategy that is prone to over fitting. Generally, the bigger the data set, the easier it is to over-fit the model.

Over fitting is mainly discovered by testing the model on one or more than one new set of data. If it is found that the data is over fitted, then the model will fail with the new data. It can be tragic to spend months or years for the development of a model that better works like a pro for training data and for the first set of test data, but completely fails for a new set of data.

7.3. BIGNESS BIAS

As Big Data methods use huge sets of data, there is a trend to give the outcome more confidence than would be given to a set of outcomes produced from a small set of data. Well, this is a mistaken belief. In fact, Big Data is occasionally an accurate or complete data collection.

The organizations can expect the Big Data resources to be selective for the data that is included as well as excluded from the resource. While dealing with the Big Data, expect missing records, missing values, noisy data, enormous variations in the quality of records and all of the shortages found in small data resources.

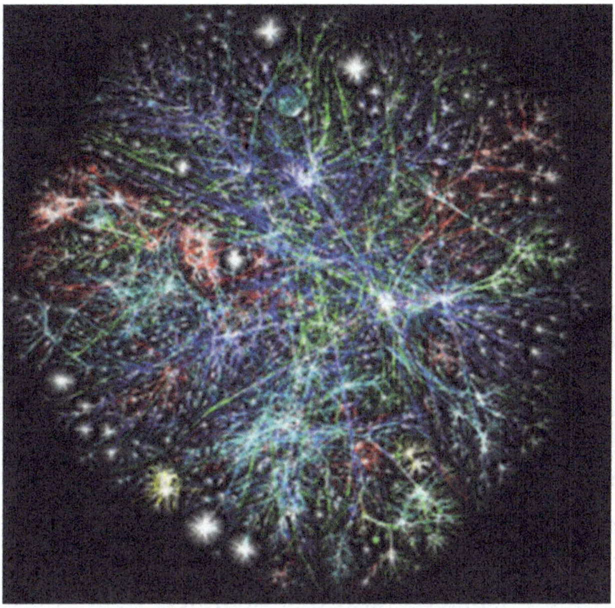

However, the belief that Big Data is much more reliable as well useful than the smaller data is persistent in the science community. Still not convinced that bigness bias is a key concern for Big Data studies. In the United States, the knowledge of the causes of death in the population is based on the death certificate data acquired by the Vital Statistics Program of the National Centre for Health Statistics.

Death certificate data is extremely faulty. In certain cases, the data in death certificates are provided by the clinicians, at the time of a patient's death, without the profit of autopsy results. In various cases, the clinicians who fill out the death certificate are not effectively trained to fill out the cause of the death form, usually mistaking the mode of death (for example, cardiopulmonary arrest, cardiac arrest) with cause of death (for example, the disease process leading to a cardiopulmonary arrest or cardiac arrest), and hence, abolishing the proposed aim of the death certificate.

Thousands of the instructional pages have been written in a suitable way to complete a death certificate. Possibly the most dominant type of bigness bias relates to the misplaced faith that complete data is a representative. Positively, if a Big Data resource comprises every measurement for a data domain, then the biases imposed by the inadequate sampling are eliminated.

7.4. STEP WISE APPROACH IN ANALYSIS OF BIG DATA

Big data refers to huge quantities of data related to the statistics, surveys, and other information, which is collected by business organizations that are either big or small. The computing of this data and analysis of data manually is extremely difficult because of which different types of software and computer servers are used in the analysis of data.

There are huge volumes of data that are being generated by businesses every day and the entire data is stored in a database. This data would consist of important information about the users, customer bases and markets related to the businesses. There are different types of analytics methods that are used for analysing data and these methods are used to discover new product opportunities, marketing segments, industry verticals and several others that would be used in the analysis of data. There are some fields in business that have problems in identifying methods and approaches that are used in data analysis.

There are different types of businesses ranging from small businesses to multinational companies that generate huge volumes of data from several business transactions and this data that is collected is termed as "big data."

These huge quantities of data are continuously stored in databases and these huge volumes of unused data may clog up the storage and databases. There is a need to process, reduce, and clean this data and the different steps in the analysis of data are explained below.

There are some standard approaches that can be used in the analysis of the data of different businesses and these approaches that are used in data analysis are explained below. The business organizations must have a clear objective while analyzing data and some of the important steps in data analysis are:

- Definition of Questions;
- Set Clear Measurement Priorities;
- Resource Evaluation and Collection of Data;
- A Question Is Reformulated;
- Query Output Adequacy;
- Data Reduction and Data Cleaning;
- Interpret data to get results; and
- Application of results.

Step 1: Definition of Questions

Before starting the data analysis for any business organization there is a need for every company to have a clear objective for data analysis and why they are analysing the data. The purpose of analysing data can be identified from any business problem or business question.

The first and preliminary step in the process of data analysis is to begin and proceed with the right set of questions. These questions must be clear, precise, crisp, and measurable.

The questions must be designed appropriately in such a way that they can fetch appropriate solutions to the business problems from the data that is available. There is a need to have a clearly defined business problem before performing the data analysis.

It has always been observed that, to ask a good and relevant question, a certain talent is required. At times, even a brilliant question cannot be answered correctly until and unless it is formulated in such a way that it clarifies the approaches by which the question can further be solved. It is always best to frame the questions in tabular form. It may be good to think regarding what actually is expected from the Big Data.

A great number of analysts usually ask general questions such as:

- how can this Big Data resource provide the answer to my question?
- what is the data in this resource trying to tell me?

These two approaches are quite different from one another, and the second way is mostly recommended to the analysts to start their analysis.

There is a need to have information regarding appropriate metrics and methods that can be used to analyse data to obtain appropriate results. There is a need to have appropriate information regarding the sources of data while collecting the data.

The process of data collection is a lengthy and laborious procedure which is an extremely important step in the process of collection of data.

Step 2: Set Clear Measurement Priorities

The setting up of clear measurement priorities can be broadly divided into two types and they are as follows:

- What to Measure? There is a need to have a clear understanding of the type and nature of data that is being analysed.
- How to Measure? There is a need to understand the methods and approaches that must be used in data analysis and choose the appropriate method that must be used in the analysis of data.

Now the question arises, is the output data categorical or is it numeric? And if it is numeric then whether it is quantitative or not? For instance, the telephone numbers are not quantitative, they are numeric. If the data is quantitative as well as numeric, then there are various analytic options.

If the data is categorical information (for example, true or false, male, or female), then the analytic options are quite limited. The analysis of categorical data is a kind of exercise in counting. The predictions and comparisons are based on the number of occurrences of features.

After the data is corrected and normalized for missing data as well as false data, the analyst will need to visualize the distributions of data. Analysts should be prepared to divide the data into distinct groupings and to plot the data by using different methods such as histograms, smoothing convolutions, cumulative plots, etc. Visualizing the data with various alternate methods of plotting may give an accurate insight and will further decrease the probability that any of the methods will bias the objectivity.

Step 3: Resource Evaluation and Collection of Data

The collection of data is the next step in data analysis, and it is important to collect data from authentic sources. The sources that are used for the analysis of data would play an important role while analysing data as the depth and details of the analysis are largely dependent on the sources of the data that are chosen. Therefore, it is necessary to choose the appropriate data sources while performing data analysis.

A good resource of Big Data provides the users with a much-detailed description of the data contents. This can be done by an index or table of contents, or by a detailed "readme" file, or a detailed user license. All of this actually depends on the kind of resource and its intended purposes.

Resources should always provide a detailed description of their methods for collecting as well as verifying data along with their procedures supporting different queries and data extractions. Resources of Big Data that do not eventually provide such kind of information usually fall into two broad categories:

- Highly specified resources with a small and devoted user base who are completely acquainted with every feature of the resource and who do not need guidance, or Bad resources.
- Prior to the development of specific queries concerned with the research interest, the data analysts should always design the layout of queries so as to assess the range of information available in the resource. A particular data analyst cannot always draw conclusions regarding the Big Data resource.

The collection of data begins with some primary sources of data called as the internal sources. The most widely used primary sources of data are CRM software, ERP systems, marketing automation tools and several others. The data that is collected from these primary sources are called as structured data. These primary sources of data contain information about customers, finances, gaps in sales and many more.

The external sources of data are often called secondary sources. The secondary sources of data are called unstructured data and this data is mostly collected from different places. There are several open data sources that are used to collect the data and this data is used in finding solutions to a variety of business problems.

Step 4. A Question Is Reformulated

Data does not answer the exact question with which the analyst starts with. After the analyst have evaluated the content as well as the design of the Big Data resource, he or she will calibrate the questions to the available data sources. After exploring the resource, the analyst learns the types of questions that can be best answered with the available data. With this kind of understanding, the analyst can reformulate the real set of questions.

Step 5. Query Output Adequacy

Big Data resources can produce a huge output in response to a data query. When a data analyst gets a huge amount of data, especially if the output is enormous, he or she will probably assume that the query output is valid as well as complete.

A query output is valid when the data in the query output produces a repeatable and correct answer. On the other hand, a query output is complete when it comprises all of the data that is held in the Big Data resource which answers the query.

> *Example of Query Output Adequacy*
>
> For example, a Google query is a great instance where the query output isn't correctly examined. When a person enters into a search term and get millions of hits, he may tend to assume that the query output is adequate and precise. When the analyst looks for a specific Web pageorans wer to a particular question, the very first output page on the initial Google query may meet the exact needs or requirements.

An attentive data analyst will look forward to submitting various related queries to see which of the queries produce better outputs. The analyst may combine different outputs of the queries and will certainly want to filter out the combined outputs so as to remove the response items that are not relevant. The procedure of query output examination is quite arduous and requires various aggregation as well as filtering steps.

After the analyst gets the satisfaction of using reasonable measures to gather a complete output of the query, he or she will still need to determine that whether the output which is obtained is completely representative of the data domain the analyst actually wished to analyse. It can be said that Big Data resource does not contain the exact level of detail that the analyst will require to support a detailed data analysis on distinct topics.

Step 6. Data Reduction and Data Cleaning

The next step in the process of data analysis is known to be data cleaning. Data cleaning is an important step in the analysis of data and the data that is acquired from authentic sources is sorted and cleaned before the data is analysed. There is a need to clean the data, remove the irrelevant data and process the data to facilitate the process of analysis which is mostly conducted with the help of a software or sometimes done manually.

The data that is collected may have duplicate data sets, anomalous data and several other inconsistencies that might affect the process of data analysis because of which there is a need for cleaning the data. A majority of the data scientists state that a significant amount of time is spent on cleaning the data as data that is cleaned properly would fetch the right results.

The availability of advanced software and tools from artificial intelligence would save a lot of time in the process of data cleaning. An irony of the Big Data analysis is that the analyst must always make efforts to collect all of the data concerned with a project, followed by a similarly difficult phase in which the data analyst must discard the data down to its basic essentials.

There are quite fewer situations in which the data contained in a Big Data resource is subjected to the analysis. Apart from the computational impracticalities of analysing huge amounts of data, most of the real-life problems are dedicated to a very small set of local observations obtained from a great number of events that are not relevant to the problem at hand.

The method of extracting a small set of relevant and precise data from a Big Data resource is devoted to by a broad range of names, comprising data reduction, data selection, and data filtering. The reduced data set that will be used in the project should always obey the courtroom oath "the whole truth, and nothing but the truth."

Step 7. Software's and Algorithms that assist Data Analysis

The last step and an important step in data analysis and it include the analysis and manipulation of data. There are several different methods and approaches that can be included in the process of data analysis. Data analysis begins with the manipulation of the collected data in a number of ways either by the creation of pivot tables, correlating the existing data with different variables and different other methods.

A pivot table helps in sorting and filtering data with the help of different variables and these tables help in calculating mean, maximum, minimum, and standard deviation of your data. The process of data manipulation may prompt to revise the original question or collect more data. One of the important methods through which the data is analysed is by data mining and data mining is known to be the process of knowledge discovery within databases. There are different methods and techniques such as clustering analysis, association rule mining, anomaly detection and several other hidden patterns that are used in the analysis of data.

There are some business intelligence (BI) and data visualization software that is optimized for decision-makers and business users to facilitate them to make appropriate utilization of data. The presence of these options would generate easy-to-understand reports, charts, scorecards, and dashboards which facilitate the analysis of data.

There are some predictive analysis methods that are used by data scientists which facilitate the analysis of data by trying to predict the future solutions and forecasts to an existing business problem and question.

There are some popular software such as Visio, Stata, and Minitab that are used in the statistical analysis of data. However, Microsoft Excel is known to be one of the most commonly used tools that are used in the analysis of data.

The algorithms are considered as perfect machines. They regularly work to produce consistent solutions; they never make any mistakes; they require no fuel; they are spiritual; they never wear down. The computer scientists love algorithms.

As the algorithms are becoming more and clearer day by day, they are now becoming more and more enigmatic. Very a smaller number of people actually understand the way of doing work. Some of the popular statistical methods resist simple explanation, comprising p values and linear regression.

When a scientist submits the article to a journal, then he or she can expect the editor of the journal to insist that a statistician must be included as a co-author. It is much easier to utilize the incorrect statistical methods that editors as well as reviewers do not trust the non-statisticians so as to conduct their individual analyses.

The field of Big Data basically comes up with an amazing assortment of analytic options. Now the concern is, who will judge that the appropriate method is opted, and implemented properly and that the outcomes are correctly interpreted.

Step 8: Interpretation of Results

The final step and an important step in the process of data analysis is known to be an interpretation of the results. The process of interpretation of results is extremely important as the results that are obtained from the analysed data would help in the growth of an organization.

The interpretation of results from data analysis must be able to validate all the steps that are conducted as a part of data analysis because of which this step is known to be a value addition to the entire process of data analysis as it summarizes the whole process of data analysis.

The data analysts and business users must be able to collaborate during the entire process as that would help them to overcome any challenges or limitations that they witness during the entire process of data analysis.

There is a need to consider three important questions while analysing data and these questions are as follows:

Does the data provide an answer to the fundamental question and how is the data providing an answer?

Does the data help in defending against any objections?

Does the data have any limitations or challenges to the procedure that is adapted?

The interpretation of the data would provide some reasonable conclusion if the data answers all these questions. There is a need to make an appropriate decision from the results that are interpreted.

The data interpretation can be classified into two categories and they are as follows:

1. Results Are Reviewed and Conclusions Are Asserted

When the person who forecasts the weather discusses the expected path of a hurricane, he or she will show different paths predicted by different models. The forecaster must draw a cone-shaped swath bounded by different paths forecasted by using different models of forecasting. A central line in the cone represents the composite path formed by averaging the forecasts from different types of models. Here, the point is that Big Data analyses never give a single and undisputed answer. There are various ways by which Big Data can be analysed, and all of them produce different solutions.

2. Conclusions Are Examined and Subjected to Validation

Validation basically consists of demonstrating that the assertions that are produced from the data analyses are reliable. The analyst validates an assertion (that may look like a hypothesis, a statement regarding the value of a completely new laboratory test and a therapeutic protocol) just by showing that he can draw the same conclusions in comparable data sets.

Real science can be validated if it is true, and invalidated if it is false. Pseudoscience is a pejorative term that generally applies to the scientific conclusions that are very much consistent with some observations, but that cannot be tested or confirmed with any additional data.

For instance, there is a large amount of information that would recommend that the earth has been visited by flying saucers.

Such pieces of evidence come in the form of numerous photographs, eyewitness accounts and vociferous official denials of such events signifying some form of cover-up. Without discussing anything related to the validity of UFO claims, it is not wrong to say that these assertions fall into the land of pseudoscience as they are untestable (that is, there is no way to prove that flying saucers do not exist) and there is no definitive data to prove their existence (that is, the "little green men" have not been forthcoming).

The process of application of this step by step method to analyze big data would help an organization to make better decisions and would help the business of the organizations to grow. The practice of data analysis would become faster and accurate with continuous practice and would help the organizations to take necessary steps in the growth of the organization.

7.5. COMPLEXITIES IN BIG DATA

The arrival of big data and the analysis of big data is known to play an important role in the growth of the business of several organizations. However, this progress made by the companies is being affected by one major challenge in the field of big data which is the complexity of big data. There is a high level of technical complexity that is associated with big data because of which a number of companies are suffering from issues such as lack of appropriate data science skills.

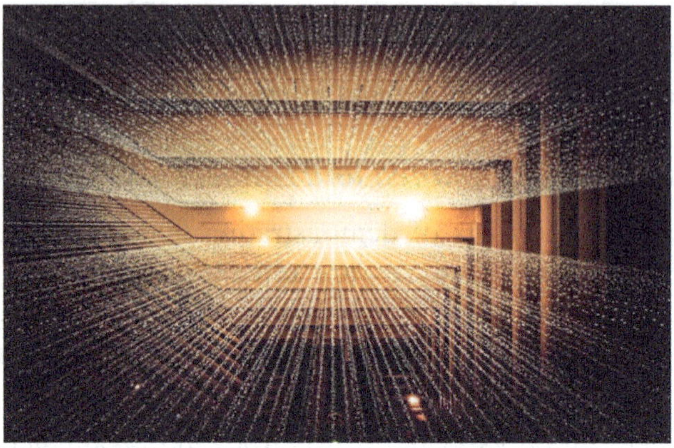

Complexity in data is also present in recruitment as there are nearly 80% of the companies who are trying to find qualified data science professionals state that it is becoming increasingly difficult to find and recruit data science professionals.

The overview of the problem in general terms instead of in detail is defined as an abstraction. It contains plans like going back to first principles or using an analogy to frame a problem. The basic logic is that the main problem emerges by eliminating the details. There are several different engines one might select to run along with the big data. The selection of Splunk to investigate log files, or Hadoop for big file batch processing, or Spark for data stream processing. The separate data universe is required by each of these those specialized big data engines, and finally, the data from these universes should come back together, and then the DBA is called in to do the integration.

Organizations are currently shuffling and matching on-campus and cloud-based big data-processing and data storage. The organizations are utilizing the various cloud vendors also in many circumstances. The data and intelligence from these diverse repositories should be mixed along at some point, because of the business needs in many situations.

7.6. THE IMPORTANCE

In the organization, in present times they are utilizing on-campus big data processing, or maybe if you're processing data within the cloud, the tendency is to easily assign another group of computing cluster for a big data application that needs its own engine or few types of hybrid processing you don't presently have. Each time you are doing this you multiply the big data clusters, and this complicates

The big data architecture as the individual is now dealing with closure silo integration.

7.7. DIMENSIONS OF DATA COMPLEXITIES

The complexity of big data is having an impact on a company in different ways. The size and intricacy of the data are some of the major problems that are associated with data. These problems that are associated with data are termed as data complexities. There can be several dimensions to data complexities and some of the major dimensions to data complexities are as follows:

- Size;
- Structure; and
- Abstraction.

Size	The volume of data. Basically, large data is more complex than small data.
Structure	The structure of data is like the association between elements. Data that is intertwined with the huge number of relationships are generally more complex than data with a single structure and reiterative values.
Abstraction	Data that is abstracted is normally more complex in comparison to data that is not. For example, a famous book containing abstractions like war and peace is more complex than a similar length file filled with primary data such as temperature readings from a sensor.

7.8. COMPLEXITIES RELATED TO BIG DATA

Data analytics has an important role in improving the decision making, accountability, and financial health of the employees in an organization. There may be a lot of information that is received by an organization regarding every minor detail such as a small incident, interaction, and transaction that occurs on a daily basis and this would lead a lot of data that gets accumulated in the cloud storage and database of the company. The process of manually organizing and managing data is known to be extremely difficult and time consuming. There are several complexities and challenges that are associated with big data and some of them are explained below:

7.8.1. Collecting Meaningful and Real-Time Data

There is a huge volume of data that is generated by every company and sometimes it becomes extremely difficult to access the right information from an immense pool of data. The collection of data from numerous sources creates problems for employees to make a decision on the quantitative of the data the needs to be analyzed. In addition, a majority of the data could be outdated data and to reduce or scrub this enormous amount of data manually may be extremely difficult.

7.8.2. Visual Representation of Data

The major objective of data analysis is to understand, analyse, and present the data in a visually appealing manner. The data is presented in the form of graphs and charts to make it visually appealing. There are a number of data analytics tools that are available to make data more appealing as it would extremely difficult to manually create visually presentable data. The procedure of processing the huge volumes of data to make it visually presentable is a tedious job and is a major challenge posed by several organizations.

7.8.3. Data from Multiple Sources

Data is mostly collected from multiple sources and there may be many times when the data is obtained from several disjoined sources. There may be different categories of data that would be available from diverse systems. The presence of data in diverse sources would pose complexities for the employees to analyse the data that is coming from diverse sources. The process of manually combining data or analysis of data may be extremely difficult.

7.8.4. Inaccessible Data

A major problem that many data analysts witness is the lack of access to data sources. There is a need for employees, analysts, and managers to access data that is present across diverse platforms. However, access to data may not be provided to everyone because of which there would several challenges in the analysis of data.

7.8.5. Poor Quality Data

One of the major challenges and complexities in the field of data analytics is known to be the presence of inaccurate data. There is a need to have proper data sources and a standard method of data analysis to make appropriate conclusions form the data.

There is a rapid growth in the business transactions at a y organization and enormous quantities of the data are being produced. The storage and handling of these data are a major challenge to these organizations as there is data missing, inconsistent data and duplicate data that is available. The presence of poor-quality data is one of the major challenges in the field of data analytics.

There may be many reasons for the presence of inaccuracies and inconsistencies in data but one of the most important reason is the presence of manual errors during data entry. The presence of these errors may lead to several negative consequences if the analysis made from inaccurate data as it would have an impact on the suggestions and solutions related to the business questions.

There is another issue related to the data which is the presence of asymmetrical data which is the changes made in data in one system might not be seen in the other system which would lead to a number of challenges in managing data analytics.

7.8.6. Budget

Budget and financial analysis of a business transaction are known to be an important part of any organization. There is needed to carefully analyse the data and provide an appropriate suggestion for the growth of the organization which involves a lot of money as the tools, software's, and employees of data analytics would involve a lot of finances and many companies may not have the sufficient budget for this which is a huge challenge.

7.8.7. Synchronization across Disparate Data Sources

There could be huge volumes of data that are present in different sources and there is a need to synchronize the entire data for better results. However, the biggest challenge is to incorporate the entire data into an analytical platform. If the data is not integrated properly then it is known to create gaps and may lead to giving inappropriate inferences with respect to the data.

The increase in data generates a need for the organizations to process huge volumes of data regularly and these organizations may face huge difficulties in processing, maintaining, analysing, and utilizing the data which is a major challenge.

7.8.8. Shortage of Skilled Labor

There are several business organizations that are facing a severe shortage of skilled data science professionals and the analysis of huge volumes of data would need a number of people. The rise in need for data scientists is exponentially high and as a result of which the need for big data scientists is extremely high. However, the number of trained data scientists is known to be extremely low and the companies are facing a huge challenge in identifying a person with the appropriate skills. There is a need for business organizations to search and recruit the appropriate talent into their organization which is giving a huge challenge to the organizations. This major skill gap is posing a huge challenge to the big data analytic firms.

7.8.9. Uncertainty of Data Management Landscape

The increase in big data and data analysis is leading to the arrival of novel technologies and companies on a daily basis. This poses a huge challenge to the companies associated with data analytics to choose the right technology that would facilitate them to reach their goal and find an appropriate solution to their problem. The choosing of wrong technology for data analysis may pose a number of challenges and risks to these organizations in terms of data management.

7.8.10. Security and Privacy of Data

The business organizations and multinational companies with constant research and internal skill development team are trying to explore the wide range of possibilities and opportunities that are available with big data. The storage and accumulation of data are known to pose a number of risks in terms of privacy and security of data.

The tools and software from data analysis may lead to the utilization of data that is present in disparate sources and because of which there may be severe security concerns and privacy issues. These privacy and security concerns are posing a huge threat to big data firms and these companies are working hard to overcome these challenges.

There are different types of corporate training programs and seminars that are being organized to overcome the challenges and complexities that are present in the field of data analysis. The industries, individuals, and specialists must work in coordination with one another in order to overcome the complexities in big data.

The big data is not so easy to learn. In spite of a large period of increasing awareness and hype, the concrete implementation of big data analytics is not broadly applicable to most organizations at the present time."

7.8.11. Big Data Is Difficult

The major roadblock in the way of big data implementation in organizations is the shortage of employees as it has been thought fora long time. The Bain & Co. survey of senior IT executives in the year of 2015 has stated that 59% believed their organizations don't have the capabilities to make sense and business of their data. Speaking specifically of Hadoop, The Gartner analyst Nick Heudecker has stated about Hadoop that by 2018, 70% of Hadoop implementation won't meet price savings & revenue generation objectives because of skills & integration challenges.

The gap in the availability of the skilled employees will decrease over the coming years however, learning the average Hadoop deployment, for instance, is non-trivial, as observed by Anderson.

7.8.12. The Easy Way Out

The organizations are trying different strategies and one way is decreasing the complexness integrated into big data build outs is by using the public cloud. As per the latest Data bricks survey of Apache Spark users, the implementation of Spark to the general public cloud has increased 10% in the previous year to 61% of total deployments in general. The cloud provides the elasticity and therefore agility in place of cumbersome, inflexible on campus infrastructure. It doesn't, however, eliminate the complexness of the related technologies.

Learning Activity

Exclusion of Complexities

Suppose you are running a firm that predicts financial trends in the upcoming quarters of a financial year of a nation. Think on whether you should consider the complexities in the data that you have got, to predict the trends and if so, why you should do so.

7.9. COMPLEXITY IS KILLING BIG DATA DEPLOYMENTS

Big data is extremely difficult to learn because of the complexities of big data. In spite of the long duration of increase in awareness and hype about big data, a concrete implementation of big data analytics is not broadly applicable to most organizations at the present time.

7.9.1. Increased Complexness Is Dragging on Huge Knowledge

The organizations are continuously progressing on their big data projects, though there are some big restrictions that are not permitting further progress because of the complexity. The big data has a high level of technical complexity that big data technology involves and also the absence of data science skills, corporations aren't achieving everything they have wish to with big data.

The latest report issued these days by Qubole, the big data as a service marketer founded by Apache Hive co-creator Ashish Thusoo has highlighted this as the main point. Qubole outsourced the task to the company called Dimensional Research, which surveyed over four hundred technology decision makers regarding their big data projects and presented the results in the 2018 Survey of Big Data Trends and Challenges.

The complexity issue of big data has come forward in many ways. For beginners, the seven out of ten survey-takers report they need to start self-service access to data analytics environments but less than one in ten even have permitted self-service at this point in time, consistent with the survey.

The organizations are trying to recruit the employees in that also the complexity is clearly being observed, whereas nearly 80% of organizations have said they are trying to increase the data science analysts over the coming years by several numbers, only 17% has felt the recruiting straightforward. The majority of organizations state that it is difficult to find qualified big data professionals.

The number of managers required to assist big data users is another indication of the complexity issue infiltrating big data. The Qubole has stated solely 40% of survey-takers report their admins have the knowledge to assist over 25 users which is a surprising number, since today's flat budgets involve admins to serve over one hundred users," the report states.

7.10. METHODS THAT FACILITATE IN REMOVAL OF COMPLEXITIES

The five methods to facilitate this are

7.10.1. Using One Data Platform

The processing of big data can take place on campus, within the cloud, or in a hybrid on-campus or cloud combination, the data finally should store on a single platform from which it is accessed. This prevents data duplications or users from obtaining completely different versions of data which will end in conflicting business choices.

7.10.2. Limit Your Active Region and Eliminate or Archive the Rest

The individuals don't necessarily need access to all the archives of old images fora very long time, as said by Dawar. It is possible the person would like access to photographs from the last six months, and therefore the rest is archived. By decreasing the quantity of data that the organization's algorithms and queries operate against, the organizations reorganize performance and acquire the results quicker.

7.10.3. Ultimately Search for a Cloud-Based Solution

The increased flexibility and agility are provided by Cloud-based solutions to scale to the requirements of big data processing and storage. There are big corporations with highly sensitive data that always like to store and maintain this data on campus, however, the bulk of big data processing and storage can be carried out in the cloud.

7.10.4. Include Disaster Recovery in the Big Data Architecture Planning

In case of major failure, there is no major requirement to go for a full recovery of data, however, the data experts need to restore the subset of data that the software applications at least need. This subset of data is what the data management experts should focus on with the cloud service providers, or on campus, if the organizations are processing the bug data in that manner. The essential matter is to truly test the data recovery to ensure that it works in the manner as the organization's experts think it should.

7.10.5. Include Sandbox Areas for Algorithm Experimentation

The users are playing and testing with algorithms for new product development, financial risk analysis, or market segmentation, the organization's big data architecture ought to have required sandbox areas wherever proofs of concepts can be tried and refined before they are put into production. The cloud is an excellent place to implement the sandboxes as it can be simply scaled upward or downward based mostly upon demand.

7.11. CASE STUDY: CISCO SYSTEMS, INC.: BIG DATA INSIGHTS THROUGH NETWORK VISUALIZATION

7.11.1. Objective/Brief

Cisco Systems is a worldwide leader in IT with many diverse business lines that leverage the power of connectivity and digitization to address customers' business needs. With products and solutions ranging from core networking to IoT, data centres, collaboration, and security, the market landscape includes numerous niche competitors and changes rapidly. Cisco needed to consistently understand market transitions and capitalize on them to better serve customers. With so much data to analyse in Cisco's core markets, especially with increasing volumes of social and traditional media, the previous methods of analysing key themes through human coding proved time-intensive and challenging.

Cisco began investigating automated statistical analysis methodologies to understand how markets were shifting, which competitors were important and where Cisco needed to be positioned. The original word clouds used by the majority of media analytics platforms provided very little insight.

Cisco needed a much more sophisticated understanding of the key market drivers as well as an understanding of how Cisco messaging was being conveyed and where opportunities existed for Cisco to be more present in the market conversation.

Cisco's Strategic Marketing Organization (SMO) uncovered a start-up in San Francisco called Quid, which has developed a powerful business intelligence (BI) platform not only to analyse big unstructured data but also to visualize it in a way that makes it easier to provide more actionable insights.

The network visualization provides more dimensions than Cisco had previously been able to understand with any automated technology. The SMO team worked closely with the Corporate Communications team to really understand who are the key influencers impacting customers' decisions.

As a B2B company, Cisco needed to think carefully about how to leverage Big Data so insights are not affected by "noise" that may not have an impact on customers and other stakeholders. Cisco started the Quid network analysis by carefully eliminating irrelevant content and focusing on key influencers. The SMO team also collaborated cross functionally to ensure the analysis represented clearly defined markets to ensure relevant and actionable insights for Cisco.

7.11.2. Strategy

IoT has been a key focus area Cisco, so the SMO team prioritized this market for analysis, using it as a cornerstone to understand the best practices of how to apply the network analysis across different market areas.

By isolating the key influencers and narrowing down to just the top seven narratives in IoT, the Communications teams saw a clear picture of what is most relevant in IoT and how themes interrelate. The network depicts security as a central narrative in IoT, clearly indicating the need for including security messaging when discussing IoT. The biggest narrative, verticals, and IoT showed a dispersed use of language, not surprisingly due to the distinct nature of different industries. Cisco evaluated each of the narratives closely to understand the key drivers of those narratives.

- The wearable's cluster comprised two sections. The more central cluster part included stories about how the Internet of Everything/ Technology (IoE/T) (including wearable's) is going to change the general industrial landscape, which bridges almost every conversation in the industry narrative. The bottom part of this cluster included the release of Apple Watch and Google wristband. Together the two sections indicated that wearable's would transform industries like healthcare.
- The largest cluster Verticals and IoE/T contained stories of how the various sectors are beginning to explore IoE/T technologies and strategies to adopt and implement relevant IoT technologies.
- Security and privacy concerns comprised more than a quarter of the network. These two clusters were lightly linked with each other and strongly linked with Innovation in Smart Homes and Wearable's cluster highlighting the importance and interrelation of these two issues.
- The innovation in smart homes and industrial internet consortium cluster was split in two directions. Google's release of a camera for Nest appeared in the denser part of the cluster. Peers like Amazon and start-ups like Nuimo also featured their innovations in smart home products. In addition, this part of the cluster was linked with the IoE/T and security cluster signifying the integration of security messaging with innovative IoT technologies.
- Conversations in the other part of the same cluster, industrial internet consortium show low levels of linkages to the rest of the network and are spread out almost vertically indicating evolving vocabulary.
- The smart cities/connected cars cluster focused on efforts to find a more sustainable way of living and how IoT benefits citizens.

After understanding the overall industry narratives, the SMO team created a visual overlay of where Cisco appeared in those narratives. The visual provided the Communications teams with a clear roadmap of where to focus the messaging efforts.

7.11.3. Effectiveness of Assignment

The Communications teams clearly understand the key drivers in the markets where Cisco competes. This has enabled the teams to develop more relevant strategies that have improved the perception of Cisco in these markets.

Cisco's mindshare in IoT has grown steadily due to this increased presence in key narratives. In other areas of the business, such as mobility, the network analysis has led to much tighter integration between the security teams and the mobility teams across all areas of the business.

While the network analysis clearly indicated mobility security held a central relevance to the industry, Cisco needed to better articulate how the company addressed mobility security needs. These new insights leveraging Big Data provide a robust, clear visualization and more agile, in-depth analysis, which gives the team more intelligence with which to do their jobs effectively.

In addition, the insights have allowed the Communications teams to conduct a more credible data-driven business conversation with their counterparts and stakeholders in the business units, which should ultimately impact the bottom line.

7.12. CHECKPOINTS

1. What are the major considerations for Big data and Analytics?
2. Explain the term 'Over fitting' with respect to Big data.
3. Define the term Bigness Bias.
4. What is the role of embracing IoT in Big Data Consideration?
5. Enlist the various steps in approaching the analysis of Big Data.
6. What are the various dimensions of Data Complexities?
7. How can multiple sources and inaccessibility of data prove to be complexities in the Big Data?
8. Enlist 5 complexities that are related to Big Data.
9. What are the various methods that facilitate the removal of complexities in Big Data?
10. How is complexity in data affecting the deployment of Big Data?

CHAPTER 8

The Legal Obligation

LEARNING OBJECTIVES

In this chapter, you will learn about:

- The legal issues that may come up in Big Data;
- The ways in which the use of Big Data can be checked upon;
- The various societal issues in the field of Big Data; and
- The issues that are addressed by Big Data Analytics in society.

Keywords
Data Ownership, Database Licensing, Copyright Infringement, Security Breaches, Corporate Transactions, Taxation, Data Privacy, Public Safety, Data Discrimination, Data Security

8.1. LEGAL ISSUES RELATED TO BIG DATA

8.1.1. Data Ownership

With the increase in the use of big data and its importance in the success of a business, one of the vital questions that are in each and every individual mind is whether and to what level can companies claim proprietary rights in Big Data. "Who owns the data?" in today's world is the most important question and it is still unresolved, whereas, on the other hand, the answer – "no one can own Big Data" may not solve the issue. Is it legal to use the data that is publicly available, and/or is it possible for one to claim the ownership rights of his/ her structured data?

Does the answer change in case when there is a plethora of data available, even if it remains largely unstructured? Is there any law, rules or regulation pertaining to Big Data exploitation in a proprietary manner? Does the protection under the various trade secrets laws help?

It is often seen that protection of data, accurate evaluation of data, as well as ownership identification of data play a very important role at the time of insolvency and crisis situations; assessing and evaluating ownership of data is a vital part in a way to determine the value of a company or of its assets and liabilities at the time of bankruptcy.

8.1.2. Open Data and Public Sector

The government of various countries and Open Data associations are putting a lot of effort in order to make the data publicly available and usable.

There are many private as well as public companies that step in into this in order to accumulate the Big Data and make it viable for various interested parties so that they can use them for innovation and for their own personal growth and development.

It is usually seen that the public sector produces and holds a large amount of data, often which is confidential and highly sensitive in nature. It is the responsibility of the government as well as companies that are dealing with a large amount of data to manage it cautiously so that the data would not misuse and use for the purpose for which it was collected.

Big Data management is considered one of the most important assets of every company, whether it is public or private, in order to effectively manage and disseminate information to the public, empowering citizens and businesses with open data and information.

8.1.3. Database Licensing

One of the major aspects in the field of Big Data for legal protection is the sui generis database right. Wherever an investment is made into methodically or systematically arranging data (which could include Big Data), a database right is vital in this case in order to protect the data legally for those that have made that investment to prevent third parties from commercially exploiting and transacting with the Big Data.

8.1.4. Copyright Infringement

It is usually seen that in the digital era, with the advancement in technology, it becomes difficult to ensure the copyright laws in the Big Data storage and distribution methods. The new Big Data search and analysis tools that could result in an infringement of the copyright in this data raise further challenges.

8.1.5. Security Breaches

Within the past few years due to an increase in the manipulation of data, the jurisdiction of several countries has setup laws and policies, which necessitates remedial action in case of security breaches, and allows the party to compensate for the loss to the person whose private data is breached. This helps in making the party liable and thus allows proper protection and security of data.

8.1.6. Data Protection

Although it is generally seen that Big Data is not restricted to data protection issues as in most of the cases, personal data plays no role at all, however, privacy concerns play a very important role in any Big Data strategy. A large number of sources feeding into Big Data, related issues such as the applicable law and data controllership cause regulatory complexities that are not very easy to deal with as there is a lack of transparency, including heterogeneous necessities on data security. The controversial areas of social data analysis and user sentiment, mixing of data and cross referencing obtained from multiple sources necessitate the need for a safe and secure legal framework that can protect both data users and suppliers.

8.1.7. Corporate Transactions

In the past few years, due to the increase in the increase in the Big Data problems, a lot of jurisdictions wake up and putting efforts to frame guidelines for data protection as they knew that their legal systems do not provide adequate guidance on the proper protection of Big Data. In any corporate transaction, the due diligence analysis and accurate assessment of proprietary rights with respect to ownership of data or used by the concerned parties, will become one of the key areas of review.

The significant growth of Big Data technologies in terms of providing software solutions and architectures is incentivizing start-ups to invest heavily with the help of financing and results in more advanced companies becoming targeted and acquired by large multi-national players.

As the importance of Big Data is continuously increasing, turning into a key asset, it is high likely that the right to access databases and ownership of data will become prerequisites at the time of entering into M&A transactions or selling assets and businesses. The total worth of business could be considerably increased where it's in reality owns, has access to and is capable of using and analysing Big Data in observance with the law.

While on the other hand, mismanagement of data may result in criminal and civil liability as a result of violations of copyright, data protection, or property rights.

8.1.8. Big Data and Open Source

It is generally seen that a highly successful, trusted, and technologically developed Big Data solutions, including Apache Hadoop, are primarily designed and running on the platform of open source software. The open source licensing limitations and provisions raise particular concerns around risk and risk assessment for developers, as well as for the users of such products and solutions.

8.1.9. Standardization

At the Big Data become global, there is a need to regulate the wants networked environments in terms of demands security and interoperability at all levels. It requires frame strategies, rules, and regulations applicable not only at the local or national level, but at the international level in order to ensure that software development, information systems, and software deployment require to meet industry standards for reliability, flexibility, and interoperability.

8.1.10. Antitrust

To the extent companies hold Big Data that are important for the setup of certain business models they can be confronted with requests to grant access to the third parties for the use of their data. Refusing access to third-party access to use any such data or discriminating licensees of such data may constitute an illegal abuse of the Big Data holder's dominant position and could result in civil or legal obligation and liable to pay huge fines.

8.1.11. Taxation

The evaluation of the asset value, ownership of data and transactional value of Big Data are yet to be framed and developed within the guidelines of local taxation regimes. A wide range of tax matters pertaining to Big Data, e-commerce, and Data Centre's such as VAT, transfer pricing, transfer tax, and tax incentives are there.

Learning Activity

Legal Implications

Suppose you want to open a business that concentrates on predicting the market trends of a automobile products and the industry, which requires the synthesis and application of Big Data. What are legal obligations you are required to make, to conduct your business smoothly, ethically, and without any legal hurdles.

8.2. CONTROLLING THE USE OF BIG DATA

Data privacy law is one of the major aspects that every business whether it is public or private should seriously take into consideration indeed in relation to the use of Big Data. While it is generally seen that these laws vary from country to country, each country has its own set of rules, guidelines, and framework for the security and protection of data.

Big Data, in simple terms, can be defined as the reuse of data primarily collected for another purpose. Among other things, such reuse would need to be 'not incompatible' with the original purpose for which the data was collected for reuse to be permissible.

Every country has set up its own policy to safeguard the interest of a person or party to whom the data belongs. The reuse is more likely should be compatible with the purpose for which it was originally collected if it is impossible to make decisions regarding any particular individual based on the reused data.

In many cases, one, and only best way to address the problem of data privacy concerns in relation to Big Data will be by way of adequate consent notifications. Effective consent in relation to Big Data analytics is not straightforward and include a lot of complexities.

The possession of a large amount of data can confer market power and exclude other players in the market. Competition regulators (and competitors) that are not granted access to use such data may attempt to deploy competition law to force such access. Aggregations of data sets during eh time of merger and acquisition activity may also bring the attention of competition regulators.

Tax laws are also keeping a close eye on Big Data projects.

> ***Example of Big Data in Tax Policy***
> The OECD's Center for Tax Policy and Administration is currently seeing a proposal (called Base Erosion and Profit Shifting) to control the way the digital businesses divert profit flows internationally to limit tax exposure.

8.3. 3 MASSIVE SOCIETAL ISSUES OF BIG DATA

Big Data plays a very important role in the growth and development of various industries from healthcare to financial to manufacturing and more. But there are various societal issues and problems that come along with the benefits of Big Data. The rapid change at which technology and Big Data are changing, keeping everyone on their toes, and the reality is that organizations and tech departments, consumer protection groups, government agencies, and consumers are struggling to keep up.

There are mainly three Big Data concerns that are discussed below: Data Privacy, Data Security and Data Discrimination

8.3.1. Data Privacy

When the 4th Amendment was ratified in 1791 in a way to give US citizens the "reasonable expectation of privacy", there was no way for those who wrote it to have imagined the complications of 21st century technology.

It is well known that Big Data powered apps and services are providing significant benefits to everyone, but at risk to our privacy. Is there any way to limit or control our personal information that is available on various platforms? Currently, we are now living in an era in which we cannot completely boycott technology. There is the need to develop certain measures, rules, and regulation in order to ensure that personal data available on different sites are fully protected. Furthermore, it is the duty of companies to protect the data of their users in order to ensure the safety and security of their users.

8.3.2. Data Security

It is experienced by every person in their day to day life that whenever he or she download any app, the app wants permission to use your data, and one always click and agreed to give right to company to use their right because one feels that the benefits of the product or service from that organization outweighed the loss to your privacy, but is it possible to trust that organization to keep your data safe? The answer to that is becoming difficult every single day.

As the Big Data continuous increase in size and the web of connected devices explodes it exposes more of our data to potential security breaches. Many organizations are facing difficulties in ensuring the data security even before the complexities added by Big Data, so many of them are drowning to keep up.

One of the major problems that every company is facing is a lack of Big data skills as there are few professionals having the expertise to handle a large amount of data, along with ensuring the safety and security of data.

One of the best available solutions in big data security is Big Data style analysis. Threats can be detected and possibly prevented by—you guessed it—analysing the data!

8.3.3. Data Discrimination

When everything is known, is it still possible to discriminate against people based on the available data on their lives? In the present scenario, companies are already using credit scoring to decide whether a person can borrow money or not, and also insurance policies issued to people are based on data. While Big Data helps businesses to provide services to customers in a better way and effectively marketing their product, it can also allow them to discriminate.

It is widely believed that customers in today's era are being analysed and assessed in greater detail and the result of that is a better experience. But what if all this insight makes it more difficult for some people to get the resources or information they need? That was exactly the question posed by a Federal Trade Commission Report, "Big Data: A Tool for Inclusion or Exclusion?"

In addition, companies should check their data to ensure:

- It is a representative sample of consumers;
- Algorithms used by them prioritize fairness;
- They are aware of the biasness of data; and
- They are checking their Big Data outcomes against traditionally applied statistics practices.

8.4. SOCIAL ISSUES THAT BIG DATA HELPS IN ADDRESSING

In the past few years, with the increase in the speed of internet and digital devices, the role of Big Data has been dramatically increased. Big data has three defining characteristics: volume, variety, and velocity. In recent years, the amount of data has increased immensely. Organizations can now collect information and analyse the information, data sets faster, thanks to improved broadband data transfers. As the market of big data expands, the scope and quality of information have also increased greatly.

Example for Use of Big Data in Social Healthcare
Rayid Ghani is the first to admit that the problem she works on are depressing, subjects like lead poisoning in children, police misconduct, and the tight link between mental health disorders, homelessness, and incarceration.

As director of the University of Chicago's Centre for Data Science and Public Policy, Ghani has tackled these issues using a combination of data analysis, problem-solving, communication, and social sciences.

The large amounts of data information cultivated and mined by big data companies can be of high importance for governments, organizations, and as well as for other entities in between. But that's not all. The amount of information collected to solve business problems and providing a solution to governments can also be used in other key areas that extend well over the realms of technology and business. Big data plays a very important role in addressing a wide range of social economic, and administrative challenges. Some of the social issues big data is going to help include:

8.4.1. Public Safety

When a law enforcement officer patrolling the streets, you feel protected. The police keep watch on our societies, immediately respond to our distress calls swiftly, and helps people in times of trouble. They play a very important role in providing safety and security to people. But it is usually seen that in most of the cases, our law enforcement officers are stuck behind their desks buried in tons of paperwork.

Although paperwork is an important task for the overall police operations, it doesn't help us feel safer. Big data opens new ways of opportunities in the field of public safety and security. The police department can effectively use big data in order to increase the safety that they provide to the general public.

For instance, the departments can make use of big data to find the correlation between the requests received from the public and the rate of crime. Law enforcement can also make use of past data, incident rates in a particular society, timings of incidents as well as the methods of crimes in order to minimize the percentage of crime. It allows the police department to make policies and engage in various decision making. For instance, by knowing a particular area in which there were most cases of crime reported, the police department can deploy more police forces to such an area to reduce the crime rate.

8.4.2. Traffic

It is generally seen that Traffic is one of the consistently occurring issues in cities and big towns across the globe. In most cases, big data applications are used in businesses for long term survival and increasing the profit of the business. However, the idea of using big data analytics to improve efficiency on our roads and reduce congestion hasn't been lost by the data scientists.

In major metropolitan cities, city planners are often trying to figure out a way to ensure a smooth flow of traffic. For a very long time, the go-to solution has always with the objective of building more roads. But that will not work always as the population is continuously increasing, this is not a viable solution at all. There is a need for a more permanent solution, and researchers think that it may be in big data. Some cities are started using Big Data to solve their long existing traffic problems.

8.4.3. Education

Big data can also play a very important role in the education sector. Universities and colleges can make use of big data analytics to improve the overall quality of education in their institutions. Big Data can be used to provide a customized learning experience to each student in accordance with their curriculum and learning speed. This can be achieved by conducting a deep analysis of the existing student data via Hadoop clusters, identifying strengths and weaknesses, as well as providing the needed assistance to overcome continuing disparities in learning outcomes. The use of big data in education can also be helpful in reducing the absenteeism rate and drop-out cases.

There you have it. These are many social problems that can be effectively addressed through big data. But that's not all; there are other issues as well that can be solved with big data analytics. Big Data provides great opportunities in various areas. All that is required is come up with better ways to deal with the instability that the influx of big data creates in our systems for better management.

Learning Activity

Social Issues in Big Data Businesses

In case, you are thinking of starting an online business of retail, what are social implications you might face in starting such a business, which may prove to be a hurdle for you? Think on such issues and enlist them.

8.5. CHECKPOINTS

1. What are the legal issues in using Big Data in the public sector?
2. What is the relation of Big Data with copyright infringement?
3. What are the legal obligations of data protection?
4. What points in legal terms are important in corporate transactions?
5. In what ways can the use of big data be controlled?
6. What are the social implications of the lack of privacy in data?
7. How can Big Data help in regulating traffic?
8. How can Big Data be used to ensure public safety?
9. Explain the legal issues that may arise in the field of taxation in the usage of Big Data.

10. What considerations must data owners take to address legal obligations in their field?

CHAPTER 9

Applications of Big Data and Its Future

LEARNING OBJECTIVE

In this chapter, you will learn about:

- The applications in the field of Big Data;
- The uses of Big Data in government sector;
- The applications of Big Data in media, transportation, banking, and weather pattern industry;
- The use of Internet of Things in Big Data Applications;
- The role of Big Data in Education;
- The trends that may be in the future in the field of Big Data; and
- The dependence of Big Data on Supercomputers.

Keywords
Machine Learning, Developers, Prescriptive Analytics, Internet of Things, Weather Patterns, Cyber Security, Traffic Optimization, Scientific Research, Banking, Transportation

Big Data has been playing an important role as a big game-changer for the majority of the industries over the past few years. According to Wikibon, the revenues of the worldwide Big Data market for software and services are projected to rise from $42B in the year 2018 to $103B in the year 2027, achieving a Compound Annual Growth Rate (CAGR) of 10.48%.

Because of this reason, Big Data certification is considered as one of the most engrossed skills in the industry.

The main objective of Big Data applications is to provide assistance to the companies in making more informative business decisions by examining the large volumes of data. It could comprise of web server logs, social media content, Internet click stream data and activity reports, mobile phone call details, text from customer emails, and machine data that is captured by multiple sensors.

Organizations from the diverse domains are capitalizing in the applications of Big Data, for investigating large data sets in order to discover all the hidden patterns, unknown correlations, customer preferences, market trends and other kinds of beneficial business information.

9.1. BIG DATA IN HEALTHCARE INDUSTRY

Yet, healthcare is considered as another industry which is bound to make a large amount of data. Given below are some of the ways in which big data has contributed to the industry of healthcare:

- Big data helps in reducing the costs of a treatment since there are fewer possibilities of having to perform diagnosis which is not necessary.
- It also helps in forecasting outbreaks of epidemics and also in making decisions about the preventive measures that could be taken in order to lessen the impacts of the same.
- It helps in evading the preventable diseases by detecting them in the initial stages. It prevents them from getting any worse. As a

result of this, it makes their treatment easy and effective.

- Patients can be provided with evidence-based medication which is identified and prescribed after doing an investigation on the earlier medical outcomes.

Example of Big Data in Healthcare Industry

Wearable devices as well as sensors have been introduced in the industry of healthcare. It can deliver the real-time feed to the electronic health record of a patient. For instance, one such technology is from Apple. Apple has come up with Apple Health Kit, Care Kit, and Research Kit.

The primary objective is to empower the users of the iPhone to store and access their real-time records of health on their phones.

9.2. BIG DATA IN GOVERNMENT SECTOR

Governments, be it of any nation, come face to face with a very large amount of data on an almost day to day basis. The main reason for this is, they have to maintain and keep various records as well as databases about their citizens, their growth, energy resources, geographical surveys, and many more.

All this data contributes to big data. The proper or correct study and examination of this data, hence, help the governments in boundless ways. Few of these ways are stated as follows:

9.2.1. Welfare Schemes

- In making quicker as well as informed decisions about several political programs;

- To recognize the areas that are in immediate requirement of attention;
- To stay up to date in the field of agriculture by keeping the record of all existing land and livestock; and
- To overcome national challenges like terrorism, energy resources exploration, unemployment, and much more.

9.2.2. Cyber Security

- Big Data is hugely utilized for deceit recognition; and
- Big Data is also used in catching tax evaders.

Example of Big Data in Food Administration

Food and Drug Administration (FDA) which runs under the jurisdiction of the Federal Government of USA leverages from the examination of big data to explore patters and associations inorder to recognize and inspect the expected or unexpected incidences of food-based infections.

9.2.3. Pharmaceutical Drug Evaluation

As per a McKinsey report, Big Data technologies could contribute to the reduction of the research and development costs for pharmaceutical makers. The decrease is expected to be between $ 40 billion to $70 billion. The FDA and NIH make use of Big Data technologies to evaluate drugs and treatment. Big Data allows these institutions to access a large amount of data making the evaluation effective.

9.2.4. Scientific Research

The National Science Foundation included Big Data in its long-term plans which includes the following:

- Formulation and implementation of new methods for extracting information from data;
- Formulate novel approaches to education; and
- Establish new infrastructure which will aid in managing, curating, and serving data to communities.

9.2.5. Weather Forecasting

The National Oceanic and Atmospheric Administration (NOAA) gathers data on a real time basis. It collects information every second, every day from sea, land, and space-based sensors. Big Data uses daily NOAA to analyse and extract value from more than 20 terabytes of data.

9.2.6. Tax Compliance

Tax organizations also use Big Data applications. It helps them analyse both structured and unstructured data from multiple sources. This enables the organizations to identify if any individual has suspicious records or maintains several identities. Hence it plays a significant role in tax fraud detection and prevention.

9.2.7. Traffic Optimization

Big Data helps in collecting traffic data on a real time basis. These data are collected from GPS devices, road sensors and video cameras. The traffic problems which could happen in dense areas can be averted by making modifications to public commuting rules on a real time basis.

9.3. BIG DATA IN MEDIA AND ENTERTAINMENT INDUSTRY

These days it has been observed that people have easy access to several digital gadgets. Due to this easy access to data, the generation of a large amount of data is certain. This can eventually be the main cause of the increase in big data in the industries of media as well as entertainment.

Apart from this, the platforms of social media are another way in which a large amount of data is generated. However, the businesses in the field of media and entertainment have realized the significance of this data and they have been capable of benefiting from it for their personal growth.

Some of the benefits extracted from big data in the media and entertainment industry are given below:

- Forecasting the interests of audiences;
- On-demand or optimized scheduling of the media streams in the distribution platforms of digital media;
- Receiving insights from the customer reviews; and
- Effective or significant targeting of the advertisements.

Example of Application in Media and Entertainment

Spotify is an on-demand music providing platform which uses big data analytics in order to collect the data from all of its users present all around the world. It the utilized the analyzed data to provide informed recommendations of music as well as suggestions to every individual user.

Another major example is Amazon. Amazon Prime that provides music videos and kindle books in a one-stop-shop also uses big data on a large save.

9.4. BIG DATA IN WEATHER PATTERNS

All around the world, there are sensors as well as satellites present. An enormous amount of data is collected from them and after that, the collected data is used to observe and forecast the weather conditions.

All of the data which is collected from such sensors and satellites mainly contribute to the big data. This can further be used in the following way:

- To study global warming;
- To forecast the weather;
- To understand different patterns of natural disasters;
- To forecast the availability of usable water present all around the world; and
- To make important preparations in the case of crises.

Example of Big Data in Weather Prediction

IBM Deep Thunder is are search project by IBM. It basically provides the weather forecasting specifically by high-performance computing of big data. In addition to that, IBM is assisting Tokyo with better quality of weather forecasting of natural disasters and forecasting the likelihood of the destructed power lines.

9.5. BIG DATA IN TRANSPORTATION INDUSTRY

Since the development of big data, it has been utilized in different ways to make transportation more competent and easier. Given below are some of the fields in which big data highly contributes to transportation.

Route Planning	Big data can be effectively utilized to understand and estimate the needs or requirements of users on different routes and on different modes of transportation and then use route planning so as to decrease their wait time.

Congestion Management and Traffic Control	Real-time estimation of congestion and the traffic patterns are now possible by the use of big data. For example, nowadays people are using Google Maps to locate the routes that are least traffic-prone.
Safety Level of Traffic	Application of real-time processing of big data and the predictive analysis in order to recognize the accident-prone zones can actually help to decrease the rates of accidents and as a result increase the safety level of traffic.

Example of Big Data in Transportation Industry

Let us take another major example of Uber. Uber produces and uses a large amount of data related to drivers, their vehicles, their locations, trips, etc. All of this data is further analyzed and the nutilized to forecast the demand, supply, location, and fares that will be set for the trips.

People also make use of such applications when they select a route to save time as well as fuel, depending upon the knowledge of having taken that specific route in the past. In this case, the data which is earlier acquired on the account is analysed and used. After that, the data is used to make smart decisions. It is quite amazing that big data has played a major role not only in the big fields but also in the day to day life decisions.

9.6. BIG DATA IN BANKING SECTOR

Learning Activity

Various Applications of Big Data

Suppose you want to open a conglomerate that operates across various verticals and uses bid data for its operations and predictions to be carried out in an effective manner. What are the various verticals you can think of incorporating in your conglomerate.

There is a lot of data that is generated by the banking sector and there is a rapid increase in this data. The prediction by GDC states that the data might grow by nearly 700% by the end of the consecutive year. There is a need for proper research, study, and analysis in the field of data science to facilitate the identification of any illegal activities that are being carried out in the financial sector.

For instance, there are different types of anti-money laundering software's such as SAS AML which us the basics of data analytics for the detection of several suspicious transactions that occur in the process of analysing the customer data. One of the popular banks which has the SAS AML software is the Bank of America and this bank has this software for more than 25 years.

Some of the illegal activities that happen in this area are as follows:

- Misuse of credit/debit cards;
- Venture credit hazard treatment;
- Business clarity;
- Customer statistics alteration;
- Money laundering; and
- Risk mitigation.

9.7. APPLICATION OF BIG DATA: INTERNET OF THINGS

Data is extracted from the different Internet of Things (IoT) devices which provide a procedure for mapping device inter-connectivity. These procedures have been used by different government and private organizations to improve efficiency and productivity. The IoT is being used widely to gather sensory data and this sensory data that is extracted is used in different contexts related to medical and manufacturing contexts.

The different application of the big data in the IoT is explained below and they are:

- Fraud Detection; and
- Call Center Analytics.

9.7.1. Fraud Detection

The business transactions that include huge claims or transaction processing would need a string fraud detection software. The use of fraud detection methods is one of the most famous examples of the application of big data. The concept of fraud detection from the times immemorial is known to be one of the most indefinable objectives for several business organizations.

In a majority of circumstances fraud is known to be discovered a long time after it has occurred and by the time it is discovered there would a lot of damage that might have occurred. The big data solutions play an important role in fraud detection and the analysis made by them are known to analyse claims and transactions that occur in real time and they have an important role in identifying the patterns of several large scale transactions and it facilitates in making real time analysis of these transactions and facilitates in minimizing the damage that would occur because of the fraud. The analysis of large scale patterns is known to analyse the behaviour of any individual user and this behaviour of an individual might change the fraud detection mechanism.

9.7.2. Call Center Analytics

There are some customers facing big data analytics that is very strong, such as call centre analytics. The data that is obtained from the customer call centre is known to be a big measure that would provide an overall understanding of the market scenario. However, the lack of a big data solution to the information obtained from call centre would be identified late or overlooked by the call centre.

The big data solutions play an important role in the identification of those problems that repeatedly occur and mostly these problems are known to be associated with the customer or staff behaviours, an attitude of staff and others. The big data solutions are known to make analysis by considering the time/quality resolution metrics and it facilitates in capturing and processing the content of the calls received at the call centre.

9.8. EDUCATION

The education sector can benefit significantly from big data applications; however, it also faces many challenges. A major challenge from a technical perspective in the education industry is that in order to incorporate big data from various sources and vendors. Moreover, the data collected has to be utilized on platforms that may not support data from multiple sources.

From a practical perspective, staffs, and institutions also have to adopt to the new procedures. They have to learn new data management and analysis tools.

From the technical aspect, there are several challenges that hinder the integration of data from multiple sources, from multiple vendors and on different platforms. These elements are often not designed to work with one another.

Another challenge is with respect to issues of privacy and protection of personal data which is common when big data is used in the education sector.

Nevertheless, big data has various applications in the education sector.

Big data is used extensively, in higher education.

Example in Higher Education

An example is the University of Tasmania which is an Australian University in which more than 26,000 students' study. It has deployed a Learning and Management System that monitors various aspects. One important thing that it tracks is the time a student logs onto the system, the time that he spends on various pages in the system. This way it is able to track the overall progress of a student overtime.

Another application of big data in education is in evaluating the efficiency of teachers. It can improve the interaction between the students and teachers. This can help in improving the teacher's performance. Based on this, their performance can be fine-tuned and measured against student numbers, behavioural classification, student demographics, subject matter, student aspirations, and various other factors.

In government organizations, an example is the Office of Educational Technology in the U. S. Department of Education. It uses big data to develop analytics. This helps in the course correction of students who are not performing well in distance programs using online big data courses. Another approach is monitoring click patterns which help to detect boredom.

9.9. RETAIL AND WHOLESALE TRADE

The retail and wholesale trade also faces challenges with respect to Big Data which has gathered a large amount of data over time. The source of these data includes loyalty cards, RFID, POS scanners, etc. However, these data are not being used effectively to improve customer experiences on the whole and any modifications observed are insufficient.

There are various applications of big data in the Retail and Wholesale sector. The retail and wholesale traders continue to obtain Big Data from POS, customer loyalty data, store inventory, local demographics data.

In 2014, a New York's Big Show retail trade conference was held. In this the companies such as Microsoft, Cisco, and IBM pitched the requirement for the retail industry in order to utilize big data for analytics and for other uses which include:

- Optimized staffing with the help of data from shopping patterns, local events, and many more.
- Decreased fraud.
- Analysis of inventory on time.

The use of social media also has a lot of potential use and further continues to be slow but it is surely adopted especially by brick and mortar stores. Social media is also used for prospecting customers, customer retention, and promotion of products and much more.

9.9.1. Energy and Utilities

There are smart meter readers which allowed the data to be collected almost every 15 minutes instead of once in a day with the old meter readers. This kind of granular data is being used in order to analyze the consumption of utilities in a better way which can provide improved customer feedback and better control of utilities use.

In utility companies, the use of big data also provides a better asset and workforce management which will be useful in order to recognize the errors and correcting them as soon as possible and this needs to be done before complete failure is experienced.

9.9.2. Smart Phones

One thing that can be more impressive can be the people carrying facial recognition technology in their pockets. There are many applications that have been used by the users of the iPhone and Android smartphones which uses facial recognition technology for a number of various tasks.

Example of Big Data in Smart Phones
The Android users use a remember app that can snap a photo of someone and then can access the stored information about any person by using their image when their own memory does not do the similar work.

9.9.3. Telecom

There are a number of various fields nowadays in which the big data is used.

In the telecom industry, this plays a very important role. At times, when operators are required to deliver new, revenue-generating services without overloading their networks and further keeping their running costs in check, then they face an uphill challenge.

The demands trending in the market is the new set of data management and analysis capabilities that can help service providers in making accurate decisions by considering the customer, network context and other critical aspects of their businesses. Most of these decisions should be made in real time by placing the additional pressure on the operators.

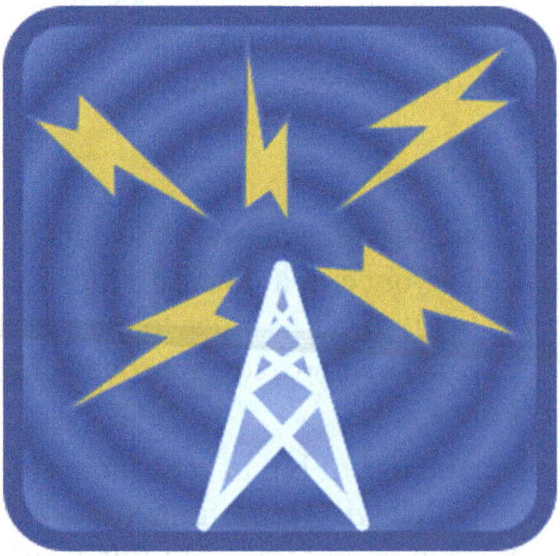

In order to support the data which resides in their multitude systems, real time predictive analytics can prove to be helpful and thus, make it immediately accessible. This also helps in correlating that data in order to generate the insight which can help them in driving their business forward.

9.10. THE FUTURE

The business experts agree that big data has taken the business world by storm, and the future will be very exciting. The questions arising are:

- Will data continue to grow?
- What technologies will big data facilitate to develop around it?

Each individual in the world will be producing 7 MBs of data every second by the year of 2020. The human beings have created an unprecedented amount of data in the last few years which exceeds the data created in the complete history of human civilization. The industry has witnessed that the big data has taken over the business in an unprecedented manner and there are no indications of slowing down.

9.11. THE FUTURE TRENDS OF THE BIG DATA

9.11.1. Machine Learning Will Be the Next Big Thing in Big Data

The machine learning is one of the most promising technology, and machine learning will be a major contributor in the future of big data as well. According to Ovum, in the big data revolution, machine learning will be at the forefront. The organizations will get support in planning data and carrying out a predictive assessments. So, organizations can face difficulties that might arise in the future effectively.

9.11.2. Privacy Will Be the Biggest Challenge

Whether it is the IoT or for big data, the biggest concern for growing technologies has been security and protection of information. The large amount of data, mankind is generating at this moment and the amount of data that will be generated later will make privacy considerably significant as risks will be a lot greater. More than half of business ethics violations in the coming years will be related to data according to Gartner.

The data security and privacy concerns will be the greatest obstacle for the big data industry and the businesses have to successfully adapt to it.

9.11.3. Data Scientists Will Be in High Demand

There will be growth in the amount of the data in the future, and hence the demand for information researchers, examiners, and information the executive specialists will shoot up. It will help data scientists and analysts draw more significant compensations.

9.11.4. Enterprises Will Buy Algorithms, Instead of Software

In the future, the business will witness a complete change in the thinking of management of organizations towards software and related technologies. An ever-increasing number of organizations in the future will purchase the algorithm and then will fill their own data to it.

It will give organizations more customization alternatives in comparison to when they are purchasing software. The individuals can't change the software as per their needs. The enterprises should change as per the product forms; however, this will end soon as companies selling algorithms will take center stage.

9.11.5. Investment in Big Data Technologies Will Skyrocket

The whole profits from big data and business analytics will increase from 122 billion dollars in 2015 to 187 billion dollars in 2019 according to the analysis of IDC. The spending of businesses on big data will cross 57 billion dollars in 2019. Despite the fact that, the business interests in big data may differ from industry to industry, the growth in expenses on big data will stay reliable by and large. The production industry will spend heavily on big data technology whereas health care, banking, and resource ventures will be the quickest to deploy.

9.11.6. More Developers Will Join the Big Data Revolution

There are around six million developers as of now working with big data and utilizing advanced analytics. This makes up for over 33% of developers in the world. What is more astonishing is that big data is still in its initial stage. So, it will witness an increase in the number of developers developing applications for big data in the upcoming years. There will be a financial incentive in the form of increased salary and developers will love to make applications that can play around with big data.

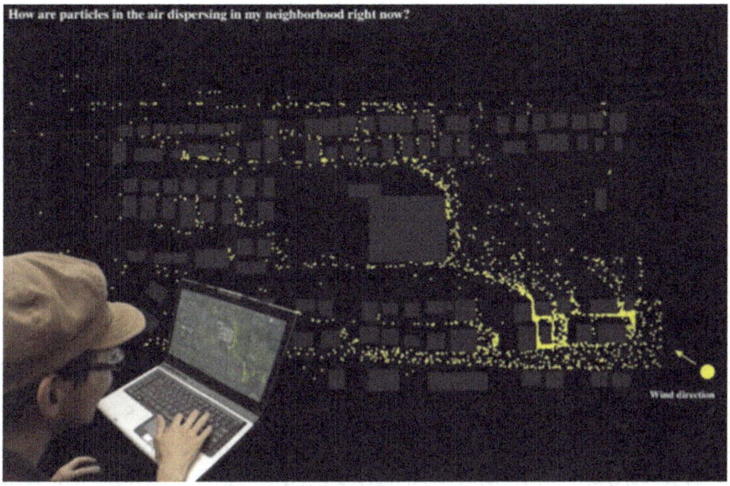

9.11.7. Prescriptive Analytics Will Become an Integral Part of BI Software

The businesses in the past had to purchase separate software for each and every activity. Today, organizations request a single software that gives all the services they require, and software companies are catering to the needs of the organizations. This trend is also observed in the Business Intelligence (BI) software and it will witness prescriptive analysis capabilities added to this product later on.

According to the IDC forecast, half of the business analytics software will include prescriptive analytics based on cognitive functionality. This will assist enterprises in making smart decisions at the correct time. The software is incorporated with intelligence, the individuals can search through a large quantity of data quickly and get the upper hand over the rivals.

9.11.8. All Companies Are Data Businesses Now

According to Forrester the increasing number of businesses in the future will try to drive value and revenue from their data.

- The businesses will witness 430 billion dollars in efficiency benefits over their rivals who are not utilizing big data by 2020, as per the International Institute for Analytics.
- According to some experts the big data will be replaced by fast data and actionable data. The contention is that big is not originally better with regards to data, and that organizations don't

even utilize the small amount of the data which is in reach to them. In its place, there is a school of thought that proposes that organizations should concentrate on posing the correct inquiries and utilizing the data they have, which can be big or small.

- According to Gartner, autonomous agents and things will continue being a popular trend, together with robots, autonomous vehicles, virtual personal assistants, and smart advisors.
- According to IDC, employee shortages in big data will grow. There will be a huge demand for experts from analysts and scientists to incorporate architects and specialists in data management.
- The latest strategies employed by companies will ease the big data expert's shortage. The International Institute for Analytics has forecasted that organizations will utilize recruiting and internal training to get their personal issues solved.

Learning Activity

Future Trends in Big Data

Try to think of a possibility in future that can have a significant standing by employing Big Data, that has not been mentioned in this book and try to think how big brands use Big Data to predict their own trends.

9.12. WILL BIG DATA, BEING COMPUTATIONALLY COMPLEX, REQUIRE A NEW GENERATION OF SUPERCOMPUTERS?

The assessment of Big Data never includes feeding a huge quantity of data into a computer and waiting for the output to come out. The data assessment follows a stepwise procedure of data extraction with some exceptions (in reply to queries), data filtering (eliminating non-contributory data), data transformation (altering the shape, properties, and presence of the data), and data scaling (capturing the behaviour of the data in a formula), generally ending in a rather simple and somewhat anticlimactic result. The most important task, the validation of conclusions, involves repeated tests, over time, on new data or data obtained from other sources. These activities do not require the aid of a supercomputer.

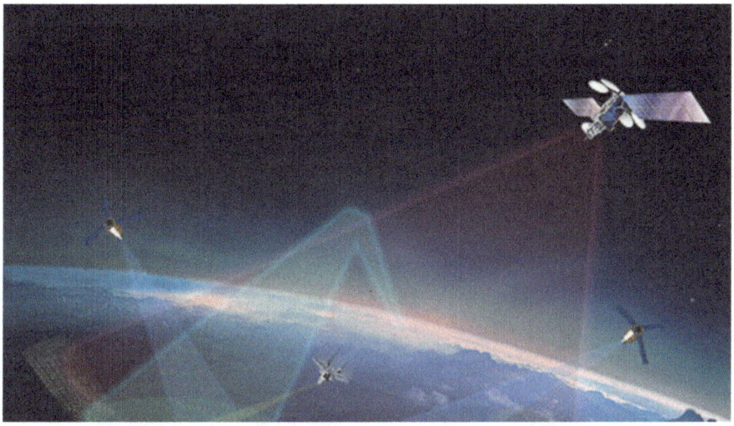

The different reports of data intensive and computationally needing endeavors on image data, for instance, Picasa and individual ratings, like Netflix ought to be received with skepticism. Some assessment methods are both computationally troublesome (e.g., requiring examinations on every single imaginable blend of information esteems) and exceptionally iterative (example needing reiterations over a large amount of information when new information is included or when old data is refreshed).

Most are not one or the other. At the point when a logical procedure takes quite a while (i.e., numerous hours), the probability is that the analyst have picked a wrong algorithm or which is not required or they have opted for assessing a complete data set when a representative sampling with the decreased set of variables would get the job done.

In spite of the fact that moving up to a supercomputer or parallelizing the calculation over a large variety of computers is a suitable choice for well-supported and well-staffed ventures, it need not be essential. In simple terms re-examining the issue will frequently prompt a methodology fit to a personal computer.

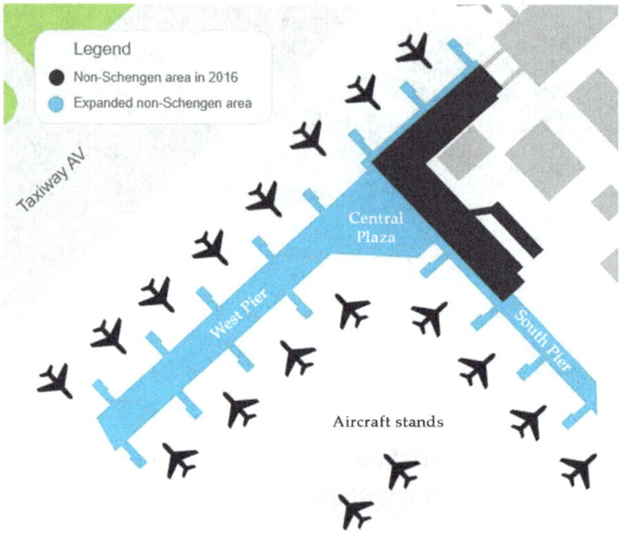

The desktop computers are turning significantly more dominant than they really should be for most analytical interests. Desktop computers in 2012, utilizing top-performance graphics processing units, could work at around two teraflops that is two trillion floating point operations per second. It is about a similar speed as the top class supercomputers built in the year 2000. In the beginning, it was structured only for games and projects that involve the graphics, graphics processing units but at present can assist standard programming tasks.

In other situations, if big data analytics no longer need the utilization of supercomputers, why try putting resources into the expense of building up these machines? There are a few reasons. Presumably, the most significant reason is that building quicker and all the more powerful supercomputers are the thing that scientists have completed very successfully.

The top supercomputers at present on the planet attain a speed of around 20 petaflops (20 thousand trillion operations per second). Besides that, there are a number of issues for which highly exact or specific solutions are required. There are some of these arrangements that have incredible scientific, political, or economic significance. Some of the examples are weather forecasting (example, long-range, and global prediction), simulations of nuclear weapons, decryption, and dynamic molecular modeling, like protein folding, Big Bang expansion, supernova events, complex chemical reactions).

7.13. CONCLUSION

From the information given above about Big Data, it is quite evident that this field has had a big role to play in the field of analysis and BI. The amount of data is being generated at an extremely rapid pace and from a wide range of devices such as mobile phones, machine logs, social media and various other sources in the surroundings. The volume of the data is growing in an exponential way and it is additionally being promoted by the growth of new technologies such as the IoT and so on.

There are various tools to deal with such data that help in structuring the data and then processing it. The data is integrated in a certain way to be used for analysis and it is further reduced in a proper manner. There are several approaches that can be employed in the field of Big Data Analysis and some complexities that need to be dealt with. There are certain legal obligations as well as social problems that need to be focused on, for better understanding.

9.14. CHECKPOINTS

1. List the various applications of Big Data in the government sector
2. How can Big Data be employed in Media and entertainment industry?
3. In what ways can Big Data help in conducting operations in the transportation industry?
4. Why is Big Data used widely in the Banking sector?
5. How can Big Data help to improve the education sector?
6. How can Big Data pose some challenges in the future?
7. In what ways will BI aid the business world through Big Data?
8. What can be the positive attributes of Big Data in the future?
9. What can be a predicted role of supercomputers in the field of Big Data?
10. How can Big Data aid in predicting weather patterns?

INDEX

S

T

U

V

W

Printed in the United States
By Bookmasters